Allen Roberts

THE TURNING POINT

The Assassination of Louis Barthou and King Alexander I of Yugoslavia

ST. MARTIN'S PRESS / New York

This book is dedicated to my wife, Mildred, whose encouragement and help was of so great a service to me.

Contents

The Turning Point

1 The Ustacha

A large box stood on a bare wooden table in a room in a house in the middle of Europe. Nervous hands reached toward the box; nervous eyes were averted or covered. Each hand drew back clutching either a white cube or a black one. Three black cubes determined the winners of this fearful lottery, as members of the dread Ustacha terrorist organization laid their plans for an assault upon the course of history.

It was early September 1934; the place was the property of the People's Saving Bank, an apartment building at No. 23 Hortz-Miklos-Ut in the town of Nagy Kanitza, Hungary. Dr. Joseph Kreisler, an attorney who also served the Bank as renting agent for the building, had leased the apartment to one Emil Horvat. The real name of the new tenant was Gustave Perchets, and he was an Ustacha.

The occupants of the apartment had come to Nagy Kanitza

from Yanka Pusta, an Ustacha training camp where they had been taught by experts to shoot and throw bombs. They had hardly settled into their new quarters when they were asked to play the deadly game of chance. The men who picked the black cubes were told that fate had chosen them to help liberate Croatia by murdering King Alexander of Yugoslavia.

The lucky gamblers were Zvonomir Pospishil, Mio Kral, and Yvan Raich. The three were happy to have the honor of killing a man they considered to be the enemy of the Croatian people. They repeated aloud the oath they had taken when they were enrolled in the organization, which ended: "Failing my oath, I shall accept death as the penalty, God help me, Amen!"

While these Ustacha were drawing lots in their game of murder, their fellow members in North Italy were also preparing themselves for the same objective. The most vicious man among them—the bodyguard of the leader, Ante Pavelich—was to take a leading part in the assassination of Alexander. A native of Macedonia, he had used many false names during his long and bloody career as a gunman. He had been called Georgiev, Stoyanov, Dimitrov, Chernozemsly, Suk, Kerin, Keleman, and Velichko in his time. His close friends, however, called him Vlada the Chauffeur.

Vlada the Chauffeur looked like a murderer. His ugly, Tartar-like countenance with its gleaming teeth was a nightmare come to life. His large brown eyes were like pieces of flint, with hardly a trace of human kindness. His mouth was a razor-thin slit, and his immense size intimidated everybody who came across him. He was only thirty-seven years old when chosen to kill the King. An experienced man with a gun or a bomb, when provoked he liked to use his fists to subdue an antagonist.

Vlada was an illiterate, hardly able to converse intelligently in his native tongue. His language was Bulgarian and his vocabularly probably did not exceed two hundred words. He may not have been an intellectual, but he was an excellent tutor, and his loyalty to Pavelich was of the unquestioning kind. Vlada had been appointed supervisor of the department of bomb-throwing and sharpshooting in the school that was being conducted by the Ustacha in North Italy. He also taught his pupils how to conduct raids on defenseless farmers in southern Serbia.

One of Vlada's most promising students had been Peter Oreb, a tall, tough peasant lad from an island off the Dalmatian coast. Oreb had been making a mean living as a smuggler of sugar and silk. He was accustomed to facing danger. Border guards frequently took potshots at him as he crossed the frontier with his contraband. He had led a very hard life. In December of 1933, however, Oreb and two assistants—Pogorelets and Begovich—had been chosen to kill King Alexander in Zagreb's Yevachich Square.

Posing as skiers, the three had glided their way to the Julian Alps and crossed the border into Slovenia, where they took a train for Zagreb. They had Hungarian passports and two thousand dinars. Ante Pavelich had promised that they would receive a huge reward after accomplishing their mission. Here was sudden opportunity for Oreb: a chance to try for a reward amounting to half a million lire, enough money to marry, have children, and live in comfort for years to come.

Alexander went to Croatia planning to stay at the palace of the provincial governor in Zagreb. He intended to see Archbishop Bauer, the Catholic Metropolitan. He and Queen Marie would then attend services in the Cathedral of St. Stephen.

The royal couple arrived on schedule in the Croatian capital. They were driven through the streets of Zagreb early the next morning. Thousands of cheering Croats lined the streets. Oreb was in the crowd. He had been told by Pavelich that the Croats had no love for their monarch. He was surprised to see how enthusiastic they appeared to be as Alexander was driven by.

Oreb was standing near the King's car, on the Square. Begovich and Pogorelets were on the opposite side of the Square. Oreb had been told to throw the first bomb. If that attempt failed, his associates were to toss another two bombs. But the inexperienced Oreb lost his nerve at the last moment. He stood still and did nothing at all.

The car stopped in front of the Cathedral; Alexander and his Queen stepped out. They were given the traditional blessing by Archbishop Bauer. Oreb, standing a few hundred feet from the monarch, could have tossed a bomb and killed him. But that would have entailed murdering a Catholic prelate, which Oreb, a devout believer, could not bring himself to do.

Inside the Cathedral the organist began to play special music for the occasion. Alexander and Marie walked down the aisle with measured steps. It was now too late to throw a bomb: hundreds of Croats would be killed. Oreb ran out of the Cathedral. His two comrades were waiting for him in the street. The three men had a furious argument, to which Oreb finally called a halt because they were attracting too much attention from the natives. They walked to the house of a secret Ustacha leader.

The police had been informed that three assassins were in town. Knowing that a man named Herentich was the chief of the local Ustacha, they decided to raid his house the next day. No one ever explained why they waited a day before they staged the raid.

When the gendarmes finally rang Herentich's doorbell, he engaged them in a long conversation. One finally became impatient, brushed past the Ustacha, and entered the house. The bedroom door was shut tight; the gendarme ordered that it be opened. When no one moved to act, he broke down the door and found himself confronted by the three terrorists. Oreb fired at the gendarme, who fell wounded to the floor. The assassins ran into the street, the wounded gendarme crawling after them. He managed to reach the police car, and ordered the driver—sitting quietly at the wheel—to start up and pursue the escaping Ustacha. The police never explained why the driver was sitting so peacefully while murderers were on the loose.

Begovich and Pogorelets were caught within a few minutes, but Oreb, a very fast runner, was able to make good his getaway. He caught up with a trolley car and stayed on until it had reached the end of the line, in open country. He spotted a gypsy encampment a short distance from the main road and walked toward it. He offered the leader of the gypsy tribe money for some old clothes. He also asked him to hide the bombs and guns he was still carrying on his person. The gypsy took his money, and told him no one would be notified that he was in the camp. Within half an hour the police had been informed of the whereabouts of their quarry. Oreb was captured and taken to the Zagreb police station where he confessed that Ante Pavelich and his Italian sponsors had sent him and his two associates to Yugoslavia to kill the King.

Oreb had botched the job, and here he was revealing many of the Ustacha secrets to the police. Vlada the Chauffeur had warned Pavelich that Oreb was not experienced enough to handle so important an assignment. But Pavelich had disregarded Vlada's advice, and now Oreb was telling all he knew.

The huge reward that had been promised the assassins was still unclaimed. The King was very much alive. But the possibility remained of liquidating him when he came to Sofia to patch up his relations with his cousin, King Boris. Pavelich asked Vlada to go to Sofia and kill Alexander.

Vlada, for once, refused to go. A warrant had been issued for his arrest by the Bulgarian authorities. He had murdered an important political figure and was on the most-wanted list. Vlada knew he would be recognized as soon as he stepped on Bulgarian soil, and executed immediately. His face was familiar to the police and to most of the citizens in the capital. Pavelich did not press the point; he realized that Vlada had good reason to fear falling into the hands of the authorities.

The Ustacha chieftain, quartered safely in Turin, decided to wait for a more auspicious opportunity to eliminate his enemy.

When the Belgrade Government announced that the King was about to make a state visit to France, Pavelich knew that the right time had finally come.

Vlada was told that he had been chosen to make the first attempt on the King's life. Killing a human being was a routine matter to the assassin: he had once said, "Killing a man is nothing more to me than removing a tree."

Pavelich was determined that this attempt should not fail. There would be no more semi-trained killers like Oreb on this job. The assignment would be directed by Vlada the Chauffeur, who was a virtuoso at his trade. Three men had been selected to assist him: Perchets, Raich, and Pospishil.

The destroyer *Dubrovnik* was taking Alexander and his entourage to Marseilles; the assassins would wait for him there. They could expect to be able to kill him within moments after he had stepped onto French soil. Nothing was to be left to chance. If the first try failed, there would be a second attempt in Fontainebleau. And if something went wrong there, a third would be staged in Paris. Should that fail, another try at Lausanne would surely succeed.

But Pavelich was certain that Alexander would never leave Marseilles alive. He had no doubts about Vlada. The murder had been well planned. Every contingency had been taken into account. The revolvers, of an excellent caliber, had been procured. The killers were in practice with the Mauser and Walther guns. Someone had told Vlada that a Mauser's action was as fast as that of a machine gun. Vlada laughed and said he would need only one bullet to kill the King.

Pavelich's associate, Kvaternik, went to Switzerland to exchange Italian lire for French and Swiss currency. It would not do for the assassins to be caught—if they were—with Italian money. That would tend to implicate Mussolini and his Fascists in the plot.

Kvaternik returned to Turin and received a last-minute brief-ing from Pavelich. Vlada and Pavelich's mistress, Maria Vudra-sek, were also in on the conference. On September 26, Maria Vudrasek set out for Paris carrying the revolvers in her hand-bag. The bombs were hidden in a suitcase among her lingerie and dresses. Pavelich went on the same train but sat in a seat by himself, acting the role of spotter. If his mistress was picked up by the police, he would still be able to arrange for new weapons. He was not taking any chances now.

On the following day, Kvaternik and Vlada the Chauffeur traveled to Switzerland by train. Vlada had a Hungarian pass-port identifying him as one Rudolph Suk. Kvaternik was now called Eugene Kramer. He carried two suitcases. Vlada bore no weapons, but Kvaternik had a revolver which he later left at the Lausanne railroad checkroom. If the King survived all the other attempts and lived to reach Lausanne, it was planned that Pavelich would pick up the weapon—his personal prop-erty—and do the deed himself.

The two Ustacha presented a rather unusual sight as they journeyed toward Zurich. Vlada was silent—what could he possibly talk about that would interest a man as highly cul-tured as Kvaternik? The younger man looked like a sensitive artist. He was dressed in the height of fashion. Before leaving Vienna he had bought a very expensive suit. A silk handker-chief protruded from the upper pocket of his jacket; his tie and shirt were a perfect match. He reeked of perfume. Vlada, on the other hand, had the appearance of a primitive peasant. He was wearing a coarse-fibered suit and his feet were encased in heavy hobnailed shoes.

The two rode in a second-class compartment. Kvaternik was reading French and Austrian newspapers, full of stories about the impending visit of Alexander to France. Vlada stared out into space, amused at the thought of traveling with the elegant young gentleman. Kvaternik had been the Ustacha representa-tive in Berlin. While there, he had struck up a close friendship with Heinrich Himmler and Hitler's advisor on foreign affairs, Alfred Rosenberg. He was not a killer by nature, but more the planner of assassinations.

Vlada did not respect Kvaternik, but he would never think of questioning his authority. Pavelich had given him explicit orders to obey the young man, and that was quite enough for him. He was a soldier in the ranks of the Ustacha and had always followed orders.

Arriving in Zurich, Kvaternik and Vlada left their two suitcases in the terminal baggage room. They had to wait for one o'clock and the arrival of the Vienna Express with their comrades from Hungary. There was time for a short walk to the post office, where Kvaternik picked up a telegram from Budapest and a letter from Paris. After a quick lunch, Kvaternik and his vulgar-looking aide went and stood at the lower end of the station platform. Kvaternik held his newspaper upside down and pretended to read it, keeping it close to his face. The inner fold of the paper contained an inscription put there by Pavelich to serve as identification. There was little reason for the precaution, since Vlada had been Kral's teacher in the arts of mayhem. He had never met the rather elongated Raich, who had been living in South America for many years before he came to Yanka Pusta. Kvaternik, however, knew Pospishil.

The three men who were due to arrive from Hungary had been given their instructions and passports by Zudomir Bizek (also known as Mio Bzik), an Ustacha who served as Pavelich's agent in Central Europe. Bizek, who had close connections with the Budapest authorities, was able to get the necessary passports from them.

Kvaternik greeted Pospishil effusively, giving him the newspaper with Pavelich's inscription: "Execute without discussion whatever will be ordered by the bearer. —The Poglavnik." Pospishil read it and grunted.

Raich gloated over the upcoming assassination of Alexander. Kvaternik warned him to speak softly. There was always the danger of a Yugoslav agent or a member of the French security police lurking about. It would not do to ruin the entire project with careless talk.

Kvaternik reminded his men that they had new names. "Remember," he said, "I am now to be called Kramer." Indicating Vlada, he said, "He is Rudolph Suk, and please do your best to remember your own names."

Kvaternik had been instructed to treat the men generously, so he took them to one of Zurich's finest restaurants and ordered a lavish meal for them. As an added bonus he had the waiter bring a huge glass of brandy for Vlada. While the group devoured the food, Kvaternik walked out into the street, trying to make certain no one had followed the Ustacha from the station. Down the block he caught sight of a signal from a man who proved to be a Hungarian secret agent. The report was that a Serbian who was obviously a member of the security police had been on the same Vienna express that had carried the Ustacha to Zurich. This man had wired the Belgrade police that a number of suspicious-looking characters were on their way to France. For some unknown reason the Belgrade police attached no importance to the message.

The news almost panicked Kvaternik, however. He rushed back into the restaurant and ordered the men to accompany him back to the railroad station, where he took his two suitcases out of the checkroom and bought five second-class tickets for Lausanne. He could have traveled to Paris by a more direct route, but it seemed safer to take the long way around to get to the capital. There was less likelihood of being picked up by the police if the group sought a train that was coming from Trieste to Lausanne. The French police were probably watching the trains on the Vienna-Paris route. Kvaternik assumed the Serb had wired a description of the Ustacha to the Paris police, but this had not in fact been done.

When the assassins arrived in Lausanne, Kvaternik had them board a bus that belonged to the Hôtel des Palmiers, where they registered. Kvaternik paid the bill in advance for one night's lodging. Later that day he took his charges to a department store and bought them expensive suits and new shoes. Raich changed from a gray Palm Beach suit to a wine-colored Swiss business suit. Kral and Pospishil were also outfitted in more conservatively tailored apparel. But Vlada insisted on wearing his old clothes. He had refused to shave, and looked like a down-at-heel Chicago gangster. Kvaternik tried to convince him that his appearance was attracting too much attention and endangering all the others. But the stubborn Vlada insisted that he felt comfortable with his old suit and shoes.

Finally, Kvaternik gave up, put the others' old clothes into a suitcase, and took them all back to the hotel. When they got there, he put the revolvers in with the old clothes. Pavelich had told him to deposit the suitcase at the Lausanne railroad station, for future use of the revolvers. The checkroom receipt was put into his letter-case.

Kvaternik now decided to make the crossing via Lake Geneva instead of Lausanne, where too many border guards and police were gathered. He hired two boats, and the Ustacha were rowed across the lake by two of their local colleagues. When they reached the small town of Thonon, the customs agents took them for tourists, and they were permitted to enter France. Kvaternik took them to a café where they ordered liquor. After relaxing for a brief time, they walked to the railroad station where Kvaternik bought tickets for Paris.

Kvaternik was now able to breathe a little easier. His men had been brought safely into France, and the police were not shadowing them. Crossing Lake Geneva he had given them new passports from his never-ending supply. Vlada/Suk was now a Hungarian citizen. Pospishil's new name was Novak; Raich would be called Benes—a macabre joke. Both of them were designated as Czech citizens. Kral's new appellation was Hossek.

The passports and visas were fake, their stamps indicating that the men had entered France by way of Vallorbes. Once safely inside France, Kvaternik collected all previous passports and put them into his portfolio.

The night was dark as the train sped toward Paris. Kvaternik was quite comfortable in his spacious compartment. The other two Ustacha occupied two compartments between them. Vlada, the only calm one among them, slept soundly while his companions talked through the night.

At the crack of dawn Kvaternik told his men that they would get off the train at Fontainebleau, a comparatively out-of-the-way station where there was no likelihood of their being spotted by the police. The train arrived in Fontainebleau at eight in the morning. The terrorists got themselves some coffee while waiting for the Paris bus, due any moment. Kvaternik reasoned—correctly, as it turned out—that the police would be watching the trains, but would never think of checking on the omnibuses coming into the capital.

When they reached Paris, Kvaternik deposited Vlada and Raich at the luxurious Hôtel Regina, located on the Rue Mazagran. He took Pospishil and Kral to another hotel near the Gare d'Orsay. Kvaternik spent the night at the Hôtel Belle Vue, and registered next day at the Commodore. Maria Vudrasek and Pavelich (under the name Petar) registered at the Hôtel St. Anne. They put up at the best hotels on the theory that the law usually looks for dangerous killers in shabby lodgings.

The following morning, Kvaternik returned to the Hôtel Regina. When he knocked at Vlada's door, loud snores told him that the hardened killer was asleep as usual. Finally succeeding in awakening him, Kvaternik dragged his sleepy and reluctant colleague off to a barbershop. Vlada was still bewailing his fate while the barber shaved the thick stubble off his face.

Next stop was a haberdasher's, for a very expensive dark

brown suit. Vlada asked for a suit with very wide side pockets. Once the suit was on, he mystified the salesman by putting his hand into the jacket and withdrawing it, over and over again, to determine whether the pocket was wide enough to enable him to draw his gun with ease.

Kvaternik also bought Vlada a raincoat and a hat, which gave the now clean-shaven assassin the appearance of a prosperous if vulgar peasant. But his face was the giveaway; he still looked like a killer.

When he returned to his hotel room, Vlada surveyed his new image in a mirror. Kvaternik looked on approvingly and assured him that the change in his appearance was definitely for the better. He sent him off to take in the sights of Paris and enjoy himself.

When Raich saw Vlada attired in the new raincoat, he insisted on having one himself. Kvaternik bought one for him: Pavelich had ordered generous treatment for all on this mission. They could afford to be generous. The Italian Government was footing the bill.

Rather proud of his role as amateur haberdasher, Kvaternik took Vlada to the Hôtel St. Anne where he was inspected by Maria Vudrasek. Pavelich had ordered that the assassins should present a respectable appearance, and she agreed. Looking Vlada over, she remarked—in German, a language the ignorant killer did not understand—that despite his new raiment the man still looked like a ruffian.

Kvaternik, Maria, and Vlada went to lunch at a restaurant near the Place de l'Opéra, where Pavelich was waiting for them. Vlada sulked and looked at Maria. He had always liked blondes, and he was entranced with the woman's beauty. He finally turned his eyes away from Maria and told Pavelich that Kvaternik was a very difficult young man. To this, Kvaternik paid scant attention; he did not care whether Vlada liked him or not.

Mio Kral, Pavelich instructed, getting down to business at

last, would accompany Vlada to Marseilles. "You should know he's a dependable man," he said. "You were his teacher." The leader also revealed that Raich and Pospishil were to stay on in Paris. "We are keeping those two in reserve. If you fail, Vlada, we shall have to use them." He outlined the elaborate plan: "Kral will stand a short distance from where the car carrying the King is to pass. When it arrives, Kral will throw a bomb which will explode in a forward direction. It will not injure you, but some people will be killed, and in the confusion you will be able to escape after you murder the King. The French police will be befuddled because of the explosion. They are a stupid lot and won't be able to catch you if you keep hold of your senses.

"Remember," Pavelich said, "if you are caught they will keep you in prison for a very long time. There will be no chance of getting you out unless a war erupts between France and Italy and there is a prisoner exchange."

Vlada had committed at least ten known murders in Bulgaria. It was said that he had killed at least fifty men in cold blood. The police in his native land had always dealt leniently with him, under instructions from top authority. He did not know that the French took a more serious attitude toward murderers. A convicted assassin faced the chance of being guillotined, or sentenced to a long stay on Devil's Island. Vlada had never heard of that lethal instrument, nor did he know how deadly a place the penal colony was.

The Ustacha killers spent the next week in Paris. Pavelich, as Petar, and his Maria took regular walks from their hotel to the Café de la Paix, which served as a meeting place convenient to both the Hôtel St. Anne and the fashionable Boulevard Haussmann where Kvaternik's hotel was located. Pospishil and Kral were registered at the Terminus Gare St. Lazare, also only a short distance from the Place de l'Opéra.

The Ustacha with the sole exception of Vlada were enjoying themselves in Paris. They frequented the best restaurants and the most expensive nightclubs. They patronized the cinema and the theatre. And they found themselves some attractive women as well. Vlada's activities were confined to eating and sleeping; he devoured food like a famished locust.

Kvaternik walked into Vlada's room one afternoon and found him snoring away. Vlada had never seen a compass, so Kvaternik explained that the instrument would enable him to find his way out of the country. "Follow the needle," he said. "When it points to East, you will know that that direction will take you to Italy. Or a Southwest direction will take you to Spain." Vlada smirked. The young fool was even more stupid than he had thought. He, Vlada, had no intention of going to Italy or Spain. He planned to return to Paris and join the beautiful Maria. His leader was a fickle man, and was probably tired of the woman. He would let his loyal bodyguard take Maria off his hands. But he grunted and took the compass.

While Vlada was dreaming about his future with Maria, Pavelich was occupying his mind with more important matters. His men had informed him that General Dimitrievich, the King's bodyguard, would not be aboard the *Dubrovnik* when it arrived in Marseilles. The General had had a long discussion with the French police, who had refused to co-operate with the Serbian agents because they felt they could assure the safety of the Yugoslav monarch without any outside help. They insisted that they were in the best position to judge what arrangements should be made to guard the King.

Pavelich was pleased by this news: the French were making his task easier for him. Alexander was now a doomed man. Pavelich had been receiving reports about the French, the King, and the actions of the security services, both from his agents and from Italian Intelligence. And he knew the information he had been getting was accurate.

He was confident that his men would do a good job of work. He knew there were a number of French police agents in the pay of Mussolini, and that there was a rising French Fascist organization. He was even getting some assistance from these sources. Once the murder had been committed, they would help cover up for him. The local Rightists and Fascists had their own axe to grind. They wanted to get rid of Louis Barthou, the French Foreign Minister, because he had been making overtures to the Russians.

Pavelich told Kvaternik to talk to Pospishil, and to give him four bombs and two pistols, wrapped up in Vlada's old clothes and hidden in a suitcase. But Pospishil was afraid that Vlada would be offended. He bought two pairs of old boots and placed the bombs in them. He wrapped the revolvers in a blanket, put everything into a suitcase, and left it at the St. Lazare railroad station checkroom.

Pospishil and Raich had been told to remain in Paris when the others went to Marseilles. On second thought Pavelich decided to have the two register at the Golden Lion Hotel in Fontainebleau. There was an outside chance that the French police might decide to check the hotels in Paris. There was a very much smaller chance that the Fontainebleau hotels would be checked. If there had to be any change of plan, they could receive their new instructions by mail.

They were advised to acquaint themselves with the terrain around Fontainebleau, for they would be the ones to decide where the second assassination attempt should take place, if it were required. By this time Pavelich knew the routes the King's party would take in Marseilles, Fontainebleau, and Paris.

Vlada, now known as Peter Keleman, and Kral, whose name was now Silvestre Maly, were handed new passports, which identified them as honest citizens of Czechoslovakia.

A few days later, on October 6, Vlada, Kral, Pavelich, and Maria traveled by bus to Marseilles. They did not take a direct route into the city, but went first to Avignon, where they spent the night. Early the following morning they took another bus that was bound for their ultimate destination. Pavelich knew that the police were probably conducting a search for dangerous anarchists in Marseilles, so Kvaternik was told to rent some rooms at Aix-en-Provence. It was expected that the Ustacha would return there once the assassination had occurred.

Pavelich suddenly decided to enjoy the sights of Marseilles. He took his men walking along the famous Cannebière, past the stock exchange. When they reached the Vieux Port, he shepherded them through a gourmet lunch at one of the more famous restaurants. Vlada, eating like a ravenous animal, was a sight that disgusted Pavelich. He grimaced at the killer and then looked with concealed scorn at the other Ustacha, most of them common clods with no culture and a limited vocabulary. Ante Pavelich preferred to associate with his mental and social equals.

After the meal, Pavelich bought a map of Marseilles and a local newspaper which gave the details of the King's route of travel through the metropolis. The facts in the newspaper corroborated the information he had received from his agents and from the Italians. He was quite content now. Everything was going according to plan. After many long years of waiting, history would record that Ante Pavelich had conceived the murder and brought freedom to Croatia.

Queen Marie, Pavelich had been informed, was not traveling with Alexander on the *Dubrovnik*. She was on a train scheduled to arrive in Marseilles when the King was due there. Pavelich still did not know who would be in the automobile with the monarch. He had been told that Louis Barthou would be sitting alongside the King, and he hoped the information was accurate. An old man like Barthou would not be able to offer any assistance to Alexander when the assassin struck. Pavelich's friends in Rome and Berlin had hinted that he should try to kill two birds with one stone. Barthou was considered a very dangerous man. He was trying to strengthen the ties that bound the Little Entente and France, and that policy did not meet with the approval of the Duce or Hitler.

Pavelich had promised Kvaternik's father that the young man would be kept out of the hands of the French police. He intended to keep that promise. He told the junior Kvaternik to expect to be ordered to leave France a day after the assassination. Kvaternik was pleased at the thought; his physical courage did not match his mental abilities.

At the Hôtel Nègre Coste in Aix, Maria Vudrasek was ripping the cover off a mattress. She had placed some bombs and revolvers among the springs and straps. Now she took them out and then repaired the bedding. Vlada would carry the weapons to Marseilles. When he finally appeared, as she was finishing up her sewing, she told him that Kvaternik was soon to leave France. Vlada was no less happy to hear the news than young Kvaternik himself had been.

Pavelich, a perfectionist, had his men go over all the instructions one more time. Alexander was to travel by motorcade to place a wreath on a monument erected to honor the men who had been killed at Salonika during the Great War. He was to be attacked as his automobile was driven past the Bourse. The first attempt should be made from the eastern direction. French traffic regulations decreed that the car would be moving along the right side of the Cannebière. The crowd would probably be standing on that side. Therefore Vlada could likely stay there without attracting any attention.

Kral, armed with his bombs, would stand on the steps of the Bourse. From that vantage point he would be able to see what was going on in the street, and to throw a bomb into the crowd just as Vlada began shooting at the King.

Pavelich and Maria Vudrasek planned to stay in the vicinity of the Vieux Port and observe whether the job had been executed. Once all was finished, the pair would go to a waiting ship and return to Italy.

The conspirators held a last-minute conference in Aix-en-Provence. Kvaternik, still in town, gave Vlada a pistol and some bombs. He was the one who suggested that Vlada should leap onto the running board of the car and shoot at the King from there. Kral was told to continue tossing bombs into the crowd until Vlada had managed to get away from the scene.

Kvaternik left the meeting and returned a few minutes later carrying his suitcase. He took Vlada to Pavelich at the Hôtel Nègre Coste and the three of them discussed the impending action for a time. Kvaternik then left for Avignon, where he took a train for Switzerland. He arrived in Montreux the next day and picked up a letter he had mailed to himself, his alibi if the police picked him up.

In Aix, there were still more conversations at Pavelich's hotel. When Vlada and Kral were handed their weapons, Vlada put one of the guns in an inside pocket of his coat. The bombs and a revolver were hidden in a suitcase.

Pavelich warned Vlada not to take an early morning bus to Marseilles, as the police would be watching for suspicious characters early in the day. An afternoon bus would take him to the city with plenty of time to spare. The King was expected in town at four o'clock.

The two terrorists calmly took a one o'clock bus. They found Marseilles in a festive mood, with flags of France and Yugoslavia flying from many buildings. Vlada reminded his partner that he was supposed to stand on the steps of the Bourse, and both of them walked over there. Silence was maintained: presumably there were security agents all around, and the less they talked, the safer they would be.

The streets were packed with people. Neither of the two men attracted any attention, since they were dressed well enough to give the impression of being respectable citizens. Vlada was the first to notice that the security arrangements were actually practically non-existent. He had expected to see many soldiers. He looked for a cordon of police, but found that anyone could have run freely into the street where the car was expected to pass. This job, he gloated, would be an easy one.

The cannon in the harbor boomed. The King's destroyer was

entering the Vieux Port. In a few minutes the car that would carry the King would be moving along the Cannebière. Vlada was very happy. The enemy of his leader, Ante Pavelich, would soon be killed. Kral, without the iron nerves of his associate, was becoming increasingly nervous. Vlada, an old hand at the game, was now ready to murder another man.

Vlada urged Kral toward the steps of the Bourse, to mingle with the crowd. His hand clutched the revolver in his pocket. In a few minutes he would be leaping onto the running board of the car carrying the King, and shooting at him. The history of mankind was about to take a decided turn for the worse. The two men who might have been able to prevent the Nazi and Fascist totalitarians from taking over the entire Continent were about to meet their fate at the hands of an implacable organization.

2 Alexander and His People

Toward the end of World War I, just before the United States entered the conflict, King Alexander issued a proclamation stating his intention to create an independent Yugoslav nation that would include the Serbs, Croats, Slovenes, Bosnians, and Montenegrins.

The thousands of Serbian soldiers who had been forced to retire to northern Greece when the Austrians and Germans attacked their country were re-formed into a fighting army by Alexander and his French allies. They received their second baptism of fire on the Salonika front, and with the aid of their allies were able to break the back of the Central Powers and hasten the conclusion of the war.

The Allies had mounted a major offensive during September 1918 under the command of Marshal Franchet d'Espéry, waged by the armies of France, Greece, Italy, and Serbia. When the forces of the Central Powers retreated to their homelands, Alexander led his troops into what is now called Yugoslavia.

On October 29, 1918, the Serbian Army under the command of Alexander marched triumphantly into the city of Belgrade. The Hapsburg monarchy had collapsed in Vienna, and the lands populated by the South Slavs were free at last.

The age-old dream of a free South Slav nation was about to become reality. Bosnia, Herzegovina, Dalmatia, Croatia, Serbia, and the Voididina would all become a part of this nation. It was hoped that Bulgaria, too, might join the federation. Expectations ran very high after the war. But the stern realities of the situation in the Balkans shattered the dream of Slavic unity. The Serbian politicians learned that the peace had created new problems that were not easy to solve.

Alexander was a dedicated man. He was also a very stubborn man, and a frugal one as well. His peasant roots manifested themselves in his way of life. He had known adversity as a youth, and he never forgot it. He insisted on wearing his old army uniforms. His handkerchiefs were darned. While his father, King Peter, was still alive he lived in a small house near the royal palace, where his rooms had the appearance of an army barracks.

He had been a page at the Court of Czar Nicholas II in St. Petersburg, and had fallen in love with one of the autocrat's daughters. The young and beautiful Grand Duchess had given him a ring. In January 1914, the Serbian statesman Nikola Pasich went to the Russian capital to arrange the match. Nicholas was pleased; he had always liked the young man. But the Grand Duchess was murdered by Russian revolutionaries, and Alexander remained a bachelor for many years.

Alexander placed all his confidence in old Pasich. He was guided in all his affairs by the Serbian patriot. King Peter was a ruler in name only; he had lost all interest in affairs of state. Alexander was the actual ruler of the Kingdom. The Serbs looked to him as the head of the House of Karageorgevich to provide an heir to the throne. A bride would have to be found for him. He had displayed little initiative in that direction, for at that time Alexander had no real interest in women.

King Peter passed away during the summer of 1921, and Alexander was crowned King. Shortly after ascending the throne, he went to Bucharest to propose marriage to Princess Marie of Roumania. The bride-to-be, a very beautiful woman, was part Slav—a fact that endeared her to the Serbians. The blood of Czar Alexander II of Russia and Queen Victoria coursed through her veins.

In 1923 she gave birth to a male child, baptized Alexander. The peasants were now quite proud of their Queen. After she produced two more sons, they worshipped her.

For Marie, Alexander had a new palace erected, but its furnishings were still rather simple. The relationship between the two was a harmonious one: she was a good companion, and he was a considerate husband. There was, however, very little romance between them, as the King was too preoccupied with political matters. He had indicated early in the marriage that Marie's role was to be a mother and a dutiful wife. She was to play no part in the nation's political affairs.

Having won the sympathy of President Woodrow Wilson, Alexander had asked for and received the territories that are part of Yugoslavia today. Italy, which had been aligned with the Central Powers at first, and then gone over to the Allied camp after she had been promised a large slice of Dalmatia and other plunder, did not accept the new frontiers with good grace. Croatia, Slavic in population, wanted to be independent of Serbia; the Croats had always considered themselves culturally superior to the Serbs and did not relish being dominated by them. The Montenegrins presented no problems to Alexander: they had deposed their King Nicholas and joined the South Slav union. The inhabitants of Bosnia and Herzegovina wanted to join up with their fellow Slavs.

Many Croats had fought in the army of Emperor Franz

Josef, retaining their loyalty to the Hapsburgs until the end. When the armies of the Central Powers were defeated by the Allies, the Croats were left to drift alone as best they could. Italy was threatening to march into the area. The Croats were unhappy, but they still distrusted the Serbs. They were Roman Catholics, whereas most Serbs professed the Greek Orthodox faith. One Croat spokesman at Versailles told the Big Three that Croatia had been an independent nation once upon a time, with King Tomislax as its ruler. Clemenceau, Lloyd George, and Wilson were not impressed by this claim.

There were many different opinions among the Croats. Many of them wanted to re-establish the old monarchy. Others wanted a peasant state based on communist principles. Alexander, deciding to take matters into his own hands, marched his army into Croatia. Zagreb was captured on November 24, 1918. The Croats offered very little resistance to the Serb Army. The Zagreb National Council set up a special commission empowered to reach an agreement with the King. Alexander and the commission agreed to convene a constitutional assembly and hold a plebiscite. The Croats agreed to recognize King Peter as monarch of the new nation, with Alexander serving as Regent.

When the election was held in 1919, the King was horrified to learn how his people had voted. The Communists won 58 seats in the national parliament. The Croat Peasant Party, led by the beloved Stephen Radich, took 50 seats. The Slovenes received 27 seats, and the Moslems of Montenegro won 24 seats. The Serbian Radical Party, which was not radical at all, garnered 91 seats, while the Democrat Party that included both Serbs and Croats received 92 seats. Pasich, who was the guiding spirit in the parliament, conferred with the various political groups over a period of eighteen months. An agreement was reached at last on St. Vitus' Day. The people of Serbia and Croatia and the others in the South Slav union voted in favor of the new constitution.

A democratic document, the constitution described the Kingdom of the Serbs, Croats, and Slovenes as a constitutional monarchy, and called for the Skupshtina, or parliament, to be elected for four-year terms on the basis of general suffrage and proportional representation. Although the Karageorgevichs continued as the hereditary dynasty of the country under the principle of primogeniture, the parliament as well as the King had the power of initiating legislation. Individual Skupshtina members would be responsible only to the body as a whole, representing the people. The King retained the power of sanction, and could dismiss the parliament at any time, but new elections were required within three months and the new parliament was required to convene within four months after the old one had been dismissed.

High judges were to be appointed for life, and could be dismissed only for violation of the laws of the state. Local government—of the districts and townships—was to be semi-autonomous, under the overall control of the central authority of the state.

Freedom of speech, religion, assembly and the press were guaranteed. Important finance rested in the hands of the government, but the Skupshtina had to approve the budget.

Initiative for amending the constitution was to come from the King or from the Skupshtina. In the latter case, consent of three-fifths of the membership would have to be obtained, whereupon parliament would be dismissed and a new parliament would accept or reject the suggested amendments by majority.

The adoption of this new constitution by the people was a step forward for the country. But politicians who can put up a show of agreeing in public will not necessarily act the same way in private. The ratification of the democratic constitution did not eradicate the bitter feeling that existed between Serbs and Croats. The religious issue tended to inflame the feelings of both peoples.

The nation had more than its fair share of enemies both out-side and inside the Kingdom. There were the Frankists, who still dreamed of restoring the Austro-Hungarian Empire. There were the Bulgarians, who were looking hungrily at Macedonia and there were also the Italians, who wanted to take over Dalmatia and become the predominant power in the Balkans.

Alexander was a Francophile at heart, and confident that Paris would stand by him. He hoped to establish friendly relations with Bulgaria and Austria. But he knew that Italy and revanche-minded Hungary were his implacable enemies, never to be appeased. Given enough time, he might have been able to unify his country, might have been able to cope with the Croat problem. But in the end it was Croat intransigence, especially of those who followed Ante Pavelich and his Us-tacha, that destroyed the nation. Alexander had given his solemn promise to abide by the new constitution. Ultimately, given the troubles that beset him, the well-meaning but ba-sically autocratic ruler had to toss it aside.

Some time later, after the murder of Radich, Alexander met with a number of foreign journalists to try to justify his estab-lishment of a virtual dictatorship after parliament had been dissolved. He had received a very bad press, and the French public were confused. Why, they wondered, should one stand up against any dictatorship when the Yugoslavs had lost their democracy? The fact that Russia, too, was ruled by a dictator did not help bring the public around to support for Barthou's efforts. Alexander told one French woman journalist that he had not actually set himself up as a dictator as many of her country's newspapers had stated.

"When I suspended parliament for three years I knew that it was impossible to assemble a parliamentary government in my country. I was faced with a dilemma. I must either expose myself by assuming full authority for the period necessary, or allow things to drift and risk civil war. Civil war in my coun-try would mean its downfall. With Croatia independent, Slovenia independent, Serbia would be helpless alone. How could these little states when separated resist foreign influences?

"You can tell them in Paris that I am a parliamentary sovereign now. The people have the right to collaborate with the authorities, but they cannot replace them, for the rule of the many is not adequate in these difficult times to provide assemblies with the necessary patriotic authority."

These, of course, were protestations yet in the future. At the time of the constitution's adoption, hopes ran high all over Yugoslavia and the world.

3 *More Problems for the King*

⊏⊐⊏⊐⊏⊐⊏⊐⊏⊐⊏⊐⊏⊐⊏⊐⊏⊐⊏⊐⊏⊐⊏⊐⊏⊐

The constitution had hardly been ratified when the Communists attempted to assassinate Alexander. Drazha Drashkovich, leader of the Democrat Party, was instrumental in having the Communist Party declared illegal. The Government, however, did not confine its repressive policies to the Communists; it cracked down on all political organizations. Pribichevich, an important figure in the Democrat Party, was in charge of enforcing the restrictions against the other parties while he served as Minister of the Interior. Years later, he would find himself prosecuted for violating the same law which had legalized the prosecution of the Communist Party.

The King and his brilliant alter-ego, Nikola Pasich, had to contend with the opposition of the Croat Peasant Party. Its leader, Stephen Radich (affectionately known as Uncle Ivan by his devoted followers), called for a policy of passive re-

sistance against the King and all his works. The seventy
Peasant Party national deputies refused to take their seats in
the Skupshtina. At the height of the crisis Radich left the
country and went to the Soviet Union. By the time he returned
home he had changed his mind, and decided to participate
actively in the country's politics. He ordered his men to take
their seats in the parliament.

The King's Government included Nikola Pasich, Premier;
Monchilo Ninchich, Foreign Minister; Milan Stoyadinovich,
Minister of Finance; Milan Sershkich, Minister of Mines and
Forests, and Dragutin Koyich, Minister of Commerce. It was
an all-Serbian administration.

The Radical Party was the political arm of the Greater
Serbia chauvinists. Nikola Pasich feared the power of the
Croat Peasant Party and was in dread of the day that organi-
zation would take up an alliance with the liberal Democrat
Party.

New elections were held on February 8, 1925. Radich's party
won 532,000 votes, and became entitled to 67 seats in the parliament. Pasich's Radical Party, now allied to the Pribichevich
wing of the Democrat Party, received 1,040,000 votes, giving
it 142 seats.

The anti-Government forces had a combined total of 151
deputies out of a total 294. Without enough votes in the
Skupshtina, Pasich was unable to organize a government. But
the wily politician found a way out of his dilemma: he had
the Radich Croat Peasant Party declared an anti-state organization, and annulled its mandate. A few months before the
election, Pasich had had Radich thrown into prison. Declaring
him a dangerous menace to the state, Pasich invoked a law
giving the Government the right to arrest the Croat leader.

From prison, Radich said that he recognized the constitution as the law of the land. Acknowledging Alexander to be
the legal head of state meant that Radich had to be released
from jail; he had managed to outwit Pasich. The Peasant

Party leader now asked for a meeting with Pasich. Their conference lasted for several days, and agreement was reached to form a new cabinet. The current ministers were requested to tender their resignations so that the Radical Party and the Croat Peasant Party could organize a new government. But the two parties were ill-matched from the beginning of their union. Radich was well aware that the new government would not be able to rule the country. Pasich had very few illusions about the coalition's effectiveness, either. He planned to create a situation which would expose Radich as an irresponsible clown.

While Pasich and Radich were staging their political charades, the King decided to take the bull by the horns and create an entirely new party—one controlled completely by him, an ultra-patriotic organization supposedly above the petty dictates of partisan politics. Its leaders included all of the monarch's "yes men." Judging by their public statements, their sole concern was the welfare of the country and the well-being of the people. Most of the leaders were deserters from Pasich's Radical Party.

That old fox was greatly disturbed by the King's move. He resigned as Premier on April 14, 1926. Nikola Uzunovich, once accused of swindling the Government out of millions of dinars in a number of shady deals, was appointed the new Premier by Alexander. Pasich had a meeting with the King on the night of December 20, 1926. The two men engaged in a very violent argument. A few hours after that meeting, Pasich died.

Alexander was now the sole ruler of Yugoslavia. Pasich, who had been the respected elder statesman, was not around any longer to act as a restraining force. The Radical Party had lost its most powerful leader.

The only man who had enough prestige to command the love of all the people was Stephen Radich. But another did command a substantial following: Svetozar Pribichevich. Radich and Pribichevich acting in concert could have challenged the King and prevented him from assuming dictatorial powers. While the King controlled the army and the Royal Guard, he did not have enough strength to stand up to those two men.

The political crisis reached the boiling point by September 1927 when the national elections were held. Radich's and Pribichevich's parties won 583,000 votes. The King's party received 505,000 votes.

The victors organized another coalition. Pribichevich was a Serb, but also an enthusiastic advocate of Serb-Croat cooperation. Radich, overwhelmed by a deep feeling for the liberal Democrat, wrote a letter to his ally in which he expressed his hope that a new era had dawned for the long-suffering people of his embattled country.

"Dear Svetozar: I am very happy that after so many years we find ourselves on the same side again, carrying on the work of our youth. You and the Independent Democratic Party are the turbine, we of the Peasant Party, the waterfall. Together we will produce such a current that no man, no force, will be able to stop it."

The turbine had elected 22 deputies to the Skupshtina, while the waterfall had won 122 seats. Together they formed a majority. It was Radich who called for the new coalition. Vukichevich, the current Premier, and the new leader of the Radical Party combined forces with the cleric Dr. Koroshets and his Slovene Party, in an endeavor to defeat the liberal coalition. The Premier, suffering defeat, was enraged by the results. King Alexander now began seriously to consider Radich as Premier. But a murderer killed all hopes of reconciling the Croats and the Serbs.

Radich and his colleagues were in the Skupshtina on April 26, 1928, when the final act of the tragedy took place. Radich had proposed that General Zhivkovich be appointed Premier. In his opinion, the General was the only man who could stop the Radical Party from staging a coup and taking over the Government.

"We approve," he said, "the idea of a general as Premier. For that would mean that the King (will) obtain the position which is his due. He will be the 'arbiter among us.'

"(What will be) more natural than that the King, who is the glory of the monarchy, should become the arbiter of our destinies and make the necessary compromise. And it would then be more natural to have here a general who was not a partisan but the representative of the King."

It was rather startling for Radich, the pacifist, to be advocating the establishment of a government under military control. The democrat was letting the fox into the peaceful barnyard.

The opposition's reaction to the suggestion was powerful enough to make even a Radich draw back in fear. The opposition declared that Radich and Pribichevich were "Blood fiends! Butchers! Bashibazuks!" The Belgrade journalists called for the killing of both politicians.

That idea caught on fast. On June 20, Punisha Pachich, a native of Montenegro and a Radical Party deputy, walked into the parliament building with a huge revolver in his pocket. Pachich was a very violent man who had had a number of physical encounters with Croat politicians in the past. He entered the Chamber, where the deputies were debating the Radich proposal, and started shooting in all directions. He wounded Pernar, a Croat deputy. He fired again and killed Dr. Basarichek. He took careful aim and shot Stephen Radich. Uncle Ivan, the darling of the Croats, was wounded in the stomach. Pachich fired again and wounded Granja, and then shot Paul Radich (nephew of Stephen), who died a few minutes later.

A number of deputies finally managed to reach Pachich, and subdue him. It was fortunate that they did. At the rate he was going, hardly anyone would have remained alive in the Chamber.

Two men were extremely gratified by the slaughter in the parliament. Benito Mussolini had been hoping for just such an incident. Without leaders, it would only be a matter of time before the country disintegrated, he believed. With Radich out of the way, Pavelich hoped to win the majority of the Croats to his cause.

Alexander was grief-stricken. Radich had been an intimate friend. The men had had their political differences but still they respected each other. When the monarch was told what had happened in the Skupshtina, he went at once to the hospital, where he found Radich still alive. The King took hold of his hand. "Don't worry," Radich told him. "I will recover." The King summoned his personal physician.

Before leaving the hospital, Alexander promised Radich that he would be Premier. Radich, to the King's amazement, insisted that a military man should rule the nation until political passions had subsided. The King went away shaking his head in wonderment.

Radich was operated upon, successfully. His strength slowly returned, and it seemed he would recover from his wounds. After a few weeks he had the doctors take him back to Zagreb. But then without warning his condition took a turn for the worse, and he died on August 8. His final request was for a peaceful resolution of differences among the people of his country.

After the murder of Radich, Svetozar Pribichevich asked the King "in the name of Radich and in my own name (to) recommend that the formation of a new government be entrusted to the opposition, which will immediately dissolve the parliament in which the murders had been committed and which will conduct free elections for a new parliament." If, for any reason whatever, this could not be done, he urged Alexander to form a new government and see that it immediately dissolved the parliament and held free elections for a new one.

But the monarch gave Pribichevich's demand scant attention. While he was thinking about his next move, all of the eighty-five Croat deputies left Belgrade for home, vowing never to return to the capital. The King was caught off-guard by their action. In a fit of desperation he turned to Dr. Koroshets, and asked him to form a new government. The appointment of a Roman Catholic as Premier was a tactic to assure the Croats that they had nothing to fear from their King, who was a Greek Orthodox. But the war of words continued between the Croats and the Serbs despite this peace offering. Threats and counter-threats filled the air. The King then decided to have an army man as Premier, after all. On January 6, 1929, he ordered the Skupshtina dissolved, and appointed General Zhivkovich to head the government. And with that act he managed to destroy the Yugoslav democracy and abrogate the constitution.

Pribichevich now decided to cooperate with the King and assist him in revising the constitution. The new document called for the awarding of certain autonomous privileges to Croatia, Bosnia, Slovenia, and Montenegro.

Milan Grol, a leader of the Serbian-Democrat Party, made some caustic remarks about the revised constitution. "It is clear," he said, "that the reorganization of the state as demanded by the Peasant-Democratic coalition would not be based on the economic and social needs of the people . . . but that its purpose would be to guarantee a new and proportional distribution of influence on the part of various national groups with the expressed aim of limiting the influence and rights of the central part of the nation."

Grol was accusing the King of having betrayed the Serbs. He had been the Minister of Education in the Koroshets administration and had been relieved of his portfolio when General Zhivkovich became Premier.

The advent of a government controlled by the military led directly to the revitalization of the Ustacha. Pavelich, who had been a deputy in the parliament, was now on the loose, and within five years he would—with the aid of the Italians—become the ruler of an Italian-controlled Croatia.

4 The Future Poglavnik

Ante Pavelich had served as a deputy in the Skupshtina for several years, representing the Croat nationalist extremist faction. He considered Stephen Radich a bumbling naive peasant who could not or would not understand that the Serbs were exploiting his people. Radich held Pavelich in contempt. Pavelich in turn had a special kind of hatred for Radich.

Before Alexander had established his Kingdom, Pavelich had been a member of the party founded by Ivo Frank. Financial support for the Frankists was provided by Hungary; their program called for restoration of the Hapsburg monarchy and for Croatia to become a part of the new empire. Before the war, the Frankists fought with the Austrians against the Slav nationalists. They were against anyone who advocated an independent Croatia.

Frankism had a powerful friend in Italy. Mussolini and his

Fascists cooperated with anyone who was an enemy of Yugoslavia. Hungary also wanted to destroy Yugoslavia. She had lost a large slice of her territory to Roumania and Czechoslovakia, and the Serbs had taken a smaller area of her land. Both countries had many reasons to keep the Balkan cauldron boiling. The breakup of Alexander's Kingdom would enable Italy to help herself to the Illyrian coast along the eastern part of the Adriatic Sea. She would also control Croatia through her puppet Pavelich. That would be quite enough to dominate the entire Balkan peninsula.

The Frankists playing the role of patriotic Croat nationalists included General Stankovich (who had never relinquished his Austrian citizenship), Colonel Perchevich, Ante Pavelich, Gustave Perchets, who had served as an intelligence agent in the Hungarian Army, and Branimir Yelich. Pavelich, the most talented of the lot, had been supplied with ample funds to create dissension in the country. It was understood that at an opportune time, an uprising would be staged against the monarchy, after which the nation would fall apart like a house of cards.

When Stephen Radich died, Dr. Machek became the leader of the Peasant Party. He had no intention of working with the Ustacha. The new leader loathed Pavelich and all he stood for. He was astute enough to realize that the Italians and Hungarians were simply using the Ustacha for their own purposes, and he would have no part of their plot.

There were disgruntled elements in Croatia. The unemployed, the mindless idealists, and the Frankist collaborators were ready to join up with Pavelich and do their best to wreck the nation. Pavelich had had many conferences with the leaders of the I.M.R.O., a Macedonian terrorist organization also subsidized by Italy. I.M.R.O. bands staged many raids into Serbian territory, and managed to keep the inhabitants of South Serbia in a state of panic for years. Ivan Mikhailov, the leader of the I.M.R.O., told Pavelich that the Ustacha should stage raids into Serbia from the north while his men attacked the country from the south. By coordinating the raids, they would be able to undermine the Belgrade regime.

Pavelich's first project was to organize an army of assassins. The most likely candidates, he thought, were poor peasants and rootless intellectuals, who could be terrorized into complete submission once Pavelich had them under his control.

New recruits were inducted at an awe-inspiring ceremony. A table was covered with a Croatian flag. A knife, a revolver, and a cross were placed on the flag. Open palm on the cross, the recruit repeated an oath first mouthed by Pavelich:

"I swear before God and by all I hold sacred that I will observe the laws of this society and will execute without conditions all that I am ordered to do by the Supreme Chief. I will scrupulously preserve all secrets entrusted to me and will betray nothing, no matter what it may be. I swear to fight in the Ustacha Army for a free and independent Croat state under the absolute control of the Supreme Chief. Failing my oath I shall accept death as the penalty, God help me, Amen!"

With this fearful promise, Pavelich had a difficult time convincing Croats to become terrorists. While the peasants liked neither the Serbs nor the Belgrade Government, they were by nature a placid people. They had never revolted against the Austrians—and were even less inclined to strike out against Alexander.

But the Italians believed Pavelich's claim that he had recruited thousands of Croats into the Ustacha. The Hungarians, too, were sold on Pavelich, and handed out passports by the dozens to his recruits. The Italians were continually asking when his organization would be strong enough to wreck the Government. They advised him to maintain close contact with the I.M.R.O.

After he had started to organize the Ustacha, Pavelich went to Vienna, where he discussed his program with the Frankists and the Italians. He met with Perchets and Yelich, who had

become Hungarian citizens. The Comitaji leader, Nahun Tomalevsky, went to Vienna and asked Pavelich and Perchets to
go back to Sofia with him. (Tomalevsky, who was in on all the
secrets of the Italian agents working in the Balkans, was murdered a few years later by Vlada the Chauffeur on orders from
Ivan Mikhailov. He had expressed doubts about both organizations, and was considered to be untrustworthy.)

Tomalevsky, Pavelich, and Perchets were greeted by a large
crowd when they arrived in Sofia. A local band played patriotic songs as the terrorists were cheered to the echo. Pavelich,
overcome with emotion, delivered an impassioned speech,
ending: "Now is the time for brother Croats and Macedonians
to work together for the liberation of our people reduced to
slavery. Long live free Macedonia and Croatia!"

Shortly thereafter, a Belgrade court tried him in absentia
and found him guilty of high treason as charged. That trial
took place on July 15, 1929. It was quite simple to condemn
him, and he received a death sentence. It was far more difficult
to lay hands on him. His Italian allies protected him night and
day. He made similar speeches in Vienna and Berlin a few
months later.

Ivan Mikhailov was a man very important and much feared
in Bulgaria. The average peasant considered him a dedicated
patriot fighting to free Macedonia from the tyrannical Serbs
and hand her over to the Bulgarians. In time he managed to
incur the hatred of the same peasants because of his vicious
behavior.

When they accompanied Tomalevsky to Sofia, Mikhailov
briefed Pavelich and Perchets on the activities of his organization. Perchets was taken to a local I.M.R.O. factory where
bombs were being manufactured. Given instruction in the art
of bomb-making, he proved to be a talented pupil. Before he
left Sofia he had learned enough to make his own lethal
weapons.

Mikhailov could not stop chattering about the raids he conducted into South Serbia. His guests got a graphic description of the terror his men had created among the peasants. His raiders, led by Vlada the Chauffeur, had pillaged farms, murdered men and women, and burned down many villages.

When Pavelich asked Mikhailov what he expected to achieve with the raids, he was told that the peasants would eventually stage a revolt against the Belgrade Government because it was not giving them any protection against the terrorists.

Thousands of soldiers had been dispatched against the I.M.R.O. Barbed wire had been strung for miles along the Serb-Bulgar border. But that did not stop the terrorists at all. When Lazich, the governor of Vardar province, asked Belgrade to send arms to the peasants, the Premier reacted with alarm: the armed peasants would turn on the Government. It was quite clear he had been taken in by the propaganda of the I.M.R.O. and the Ustacha. Lazich insisted that the peasants would fight against the raiders. The Premier finally had his army officers cooperate with the local inhabitants, and give them guns. When next the I.M.R.O. raided the area, they received a hot reception, and retreated in disorder back to Bulgaria.

Quite a few years were to pass before the I.M.R.O. was finally vanquished.

Having learned a great deal in Sofia, Pavelich and Perchets left for Varna on the Black Sea, where they boarded a vessel bound for Stamboul. From that city they traveled to Athens, and then again by boat to Rome.

The travelers got the red carpet treatment when they arrived in the Eternal City. They met with a number of high-level Fascist officials. Mussolini, acting the part of a latter-day Pontius Pilate, stood aloof, directing the conferences between the Ustacha and his minions from a distance.

A lawyer and an intelligent and well-educated man—and a clear-thinking one at that—Pavelich was not any ordinary terrorist. The Fascists knew he had been a national deputy in the

Yugoslav parliament, and that he had been sentenced to death by a Serbian court. That in itself convinced them he was a man to be reckoned with. Before the two Ustacha left Rome, the Italian Fascist leaders had decided to finance their organization. It was agreed that Italy would be permitted to take over most of the territory she had been promised by the British and French in their secret arrangement before Italy changed sides in the Great War. Pavelich raised no objection to that as long as he would be made the Poglavnik of Croatia. The lawyer-terrorist was handing over all the territory from Fiume to Catarro. Croatia would become a semi-independent state. Pavelich agreed to renounce all claims to Dalmatia. In return, the Fascists promised to provide the Ustacha with sufficient funds to finance the coming revolt against the Belgrade Government.

After he had signed the agreement, Pavelich was presented with a luxurious villa located on the Viale Castelfidardo near Pesaro. He was also given a very large amount of cash and promised more. The future Poglavnik of the Croats was given an Italian passport, in the name of Antonio Serdar. Signor Serdar was to travel to Vienna, Berlin, and many other European cities on Ustacha business. The money enabled him to live in a style to which he had never before been accustomed.

Perchets for his part assumed the role of a Bulgarian newspaperman, Matthew Tomov by name. Perchets/Tomov rented a large apartment on Vienna's Wiedner-Gurtel. Taking up the life of a wealthy bon vivant, he patronized the most expensive nightclubs in Vienna and also acquired a very beautiful mistress, Yelka Pogorelets, a gypsy-like Croatian siren. Yelka aspired to a career as a singer-dancer, but unfortunately she had no talent. She was, however, an excellent housekeeper and served as her lover's secretary as well. She was given cash to pay the bills, and assigned to taking care of Perchets' correspondence.

Yelka was a Croat nationalist. She did not like spies or foreigners, and she learned soon enough that an Italian agent was

supplying the funds which enabled Perchets to live as well as
he did. The agent was the local Italian Press Attaché, a man
named Moreale. He was also giving money to Prince Starhemberg and the Heimwehr organization. The Prince was planning
to destroy the Austrian Socialist Party, and that idea met with
the approval of the ex-Socialist Benito Mussolini.

Perchets could not have afforded a decent suit before the
Italians began subsidizing him. He was now the proud pos-
sessor of a wardrobe that would have created pangs of envy
in a Beau Brummel. He drove around town in a very expensive
car. Pospishil, an Ustacha terrorist, was his chauffeur.

Perchets made many trips to Italy, where he discussed future
plans with top officials of Italian Military Intelligence. They
enabled him to get ecrasite and tolite which he used in the
manufacture of bombs. He kept the materials in his Vienna
apartment. After he had made his first bombs, he had his men
toss a few into the police barracks in Zagreb. A number of
Yugoslav police officers were killed.

Perchets was afraid of being investigated by the Austrian
police. The Yugoslav authorities were exerting a great deal
of pressure on the Vienna regime to send the Ustacha back
to their native land. The Austrians asked Perchets to be more
discreet, so he bought a farm in Klingenbach in the Burgen-
land area, near the Hungarian border.

The farm was soon a veritable beehive of activity. Striking
clocks were bought and their delicate mechanisms studied.
Perchets was finally able to get the clocks to strike at selected
intervals. Ustacha recruits were detailed to serve in a manufacturing squad. They were supervised by Franjo Shimunovich,
a fanatical member of the organization with a splendid reputation as a bomb-maker. In short order, the quiet farm was a
full-time mass-production bomb factory.

5 Pavelich and His Ustacha Carry On

While Perchets was setting up his establishment, Ante Pavelich sent agents to recruit more members for the Ustacha in Croatia, where enrollment was distressingly slow. The new recruits were given two choices. They could go to the training camps in Italy or Hungary to learn their trade, or assist Perchets in making more bombs.

One of Perchets' more gifted assistants was Mio Seletkovich. A specialist in the planting of bombs on railroad tracks, Seletkovich also had a great pitching talent which he utilized in tossing bombs at moving trains. Perchets frequently praised his protégé, and Pavelich was also pleased with him. But Perchets was unhappy. His bombs were too big, and they were not quite as effective as he wanted them to be. Finally, he learned how to make a smaller bomb that would fit beneath the seat of a train.

The Paris-Belgrade Express begins its long journey from the French capital at seven in the morning and arrives in Belgrade at nine the next morning. It travels through the night, and as dawn begins to break over Austria it reaches the small town of Villach. The train stops while a breakfast car is attached to it, and then proceeds on its way into Yugoslavia.

Perchets and his men waged war on the Paris-Belgrade Express. They generally boarded at Villach. The conductors, tired after the long journey, did not have the wit or the alertness to check what kind of men they were. They took their tickets and even escorted them to their seats. The Ustacha spent very little time relaxing. They planted bombs under the seats and then got off at Rosenbach, the last stop before the train left Austria.

Explosions on this train killed and maimed many tourists. One outrage occurred at Zenum near the Danube River, where the eminent Professor Brunetti was injured seriously and his wife and child killed. Many of the other passengers were either killed or wounded.

The Yugoslav police were a slow-witted lot. It took them several months even to discover that bombs had been placed aboard the train before it had left Austria. After further investigation revealed that the Ustacha was responsible for the bombings, the Belgrade Government asked Vienna to place Perchets under arrest. But Austria had her own reasons for refusing to cooperate with the Yugoslavs: she did not want to offend her good friend Mussolini. Perchets and Seletkovich were warned to leave the country, however, since no one could give either of them any guarantee that they would not be attacked by their countrymen. The two went to Hungary, where they continued their operations. Yugoslavia put in a claim for damages, but the Austrians had no intention of giving any of their hard-acquired cash to the claimant . . . and they never did.

After Perchets and his associates departed from Vienna, Colonel Perchevich was elevated to the post of local emissary for Pavelich. A very industrious man, he wrote press releases and feature stories by the carload, and also supplied the international press associations with pictures of Serbs torturing Croats.

Despite all the propaganda, Pavelich was still not recruiting enough men. He had to come up with something substantial to impress his Italian masters, or they might stop the flow of gold in his direction. He began to publish a number of newspapers. The *Independent Croatia*, the *Croat Defense*, *Ustacha*, and *Gritch* were distributed in the leading cities of Europe. These newspapers were also sold in the United States and South America. Most native Croats never took the Ustacha propaganda seriously, and remained loyal to the Peasant Party. Many Croats in the Americas, however, were convinced that the Ustacha was fighting to free their homeland. A number of them sold their possessions and returned to Europe to enlist in the organization, certain that its cause was a holy one.

One of the more energetic recruiting agents for the Ustacha was Branimir Yelich. He went to Argentina and other South American countries and managed to ensnare a few unwary Croats into the group. Yelich, like his colleagues in Europe, lived in high style. Yet he was still able to convince Pavelich that he was applying himself diligently to the cause.

While Pavelich was conducting his business in Italy, and Yelich was enjoying himself in Latin America, Perchets alias Matthew Tomov changed his name and nationality again. He was now Emil Horvat, pretending to be a very proper Hungarian citizen. Pavelich, with the approval of the Hungarian Government, instructed Perchets/Horvat to buy some land which could be used as a training camp. The Yanka Pusta farm, only four miles from the Yugoslav border, was a good choice. The establishment at Klingenbach was dismantled and a new operation set up in Yanka Pusta.

Life was safer and certainly easier for Perchets in Hungary. There was no danger from his new friends in Budapest—the

Hungarian Government would never be pressured into extraditing the Ustacha to Yugoslavia. They could be trusted; they were the junior partner in the alliance and had no intention of going counter to the wishes of Rome. Revisionism was the order of the day, and the authorities knew it could only come about when Yugoslavia was defeated in a war or by internal subversion.

Perchets could now send more agents into Croatia to lure the local peasants with promises of large sums of money. When they did cross over the border into Hungary, they were taken into custody by the Hungarian police and transported to the town of Csurgo, where they were imprisoned. Perchets would be notified that another truckload of recruits had been captured, and he would go to the jail and discuss their future with them. If some of the trapped peasants refused to go to the Yanka Pusta farm with him, he would threaten to inform on them. After a graphic description of what was awaiting them once they were taken in tow by the Yugoslav border guards, the recruits usually elected to accompany him to the farm.

Perchets kept most of the money the Italians gave him. The recruits, ill-fed and poorly sheltered, staged frequent riots. Their ringleaders were executed by Perchets and his henchmen.

The bomb squads were still blowing up public buildings and Greek Orthodox churches in Yugoslavia. A small fuse, timed to ignite when the book was opened, was inserted inside the binding of a pornographic book mailed to a prominent jurist in Zagreb. Officials inspected it, and their bodies were blown to bits.

Pavelich ordered arsenals set up throughout Croatia and Dalmatia. Guns, bombs, and other weapons were transported in flat-bottomed boats on the Drava River. The Yugoslav border and river patrols tried to stop this traffic in arms, but many of the boats eluded them. One of the chief gun runners was a

South American named Korbot. He was killed when his boat blew up accidentally.

Pavelich had talked about an impending uprising for so long that he finally managed to convince himself that thousands of Croats, Slovenes, and Bosnians were just waiting for him to give the signal to start the revolt. He had a few hundred followers in Croatia and had recruited a few dozen Dalmatians and Montenegrins. The majority of the Croats and other ethnic groups living in Yugoslavia knew that the Ustacha was supported by the Italians, and that was enough to dissuade them from joining up.

But if Pavelich could not convince the Croats that he represented the wave of the future, he was still able to keep the Italians won over. Mussolini personally had ordered the building of an Ustacha camp in Zara. The Italian military had been commanded to train a small group of Dalmatians and Montenegrins who had enrolled.

These men had been simple fishermen and farmers before they became members of the terrorist society. The more sophisticated among them accepted the Italian money and arms, but they had no intention of fighting for Pavelich. They sold the guns to hunters and then came back to the Italian camp and asked for more. Mussolini's agents began to believe that they were making progress, and distributed more rifles to them. Enough weapons were handed out to start a small-scale war. But the peasants were not going to war. They were selling the weapons for a hundred dinars apiece and getting rich in the process.

Under these conditions, a revolt against the Government was set in motion. Two hundred men dressed in Ustacha uniforms, all armed to the teeth, attacked a Coast Guard installation and captured it. They confiscated donkeys from the local peasants and used them to carry ammunition and food. There was no resistance at the beginning of the attack. Ustacha shouts

of "Long Live Dalmatia—Long Live Independent Croatia"
made no impression on the phlegmatic peasants. But when the
raiders arrived in the town of Gospich, they were repelled by
well-armed police and local manpower. The would-be con-
querors retreated in disorder. The loyalists captured several
cases of explosives and a huge haul of Italian cartridges.

Pavelich's forces were a seedy-looking lot when they finally
reached Zara. They were immediately sent to Fiume, and
from there to the Ustacha camp at Borgotaro.

The raids and the frequent bombings did not create the expected chaos in Yugoslavia. But they did alarm the Belgrade
Government. The King was not the kind of man to be frightened. His security police, however, knew that the Ustacha
would stage more raids. They were sure that the terrorists
would continue to search for a way to kill the monarch; steps
had to be taken to safeguard him. Wherever Alexander was
scheduled to make an appearance, the police saw to it that
all windows and doors of the houses were shut tight. An agent
or policeman was posted every two feet along the route he
was expected to take.

Alexander realized that he was facing possible death on his
trip to Sofia. Before his departure he attempted to calm his
fears by visiting Franyo Bastel, a famous astrologer who lived
in Zagreb. The seer told him that he would be murdered in
1934. The King also received a very old woman who told him
that she had had a dream. In this dream, his father had told
her that the son he loved so well would be covered with
blood. The old King Peter had then instructed her to go to
Alexander and warn him that he was in grave danger. The old
woman, a devout Catholic, had previously revealed this dream
to her confessor, who had told her to see the King and impart
to him what she had dreamed. The monarch listened to what
she had to say, and gave her a substantial reward.

The Yugoslavian King knew that he was living on borrowed
time. But he regarded the danger he faced daily as an occupa-

tional hazard. He hoped that he would be able to create a viable state before he died. He did manage to keep the Croats and Serbs from slaughtering each other while he was alive—and that was an accomplishment of sorts.

Pavelich's men attacked the 54th Yugoslav Infantry Regiment barracks in Split; nevertheless there was still no mass uprising. The Fascists began to show their impatience. They had sunk a great amount of money into the venture, and the results were not commensurate with the investment. Pavelich paid a hurried visit to Yanka Pusta. He had been told that a large group of Ustacha fully equipped with bombs and rifles were about to cross the Hungarian border into Croatia. Arriving at the farm, he could discover only forty-five sorry-looking recruits. He exhorted the bedraggled lot that the people of Croatia were about to revolt. But nothing seemed to move the masses across the border. Pavelich worked himself into a state of complete despair. He had accustomed himself to his new mode of living. The once poverty-stricken lawyer was now a man of means—but all would vanish overnight if Mussolini learned that the Ustacha did not amount to anything in Yugoslavia. Pavelich's newspapers continued to print propaganda about the brave exploits of his men in Croatia, but the Italians wanted action. Their trained journalists could write their own stories.

Just when Pavelich's fortunes were at a low ebb, another problem came up to haunt him. Perchets killed an Ustacha who had attempted to escape from Yanka Pusta. Other Ustacha led by Seletkovich staged a mutiny. Perchets ordered the execution of Seletkovich, but the guns were turned on Perchets, who barely managed to reach his car unharmed. When he got to Budapest he contacted the police, who sent a small group of Hungarian soldiers to the farm to restore order.

Perchets obtained a fresh Hungarian passport and changed his name to Joseph Steiner. He rented an apartment in Budapest and told his mistress, Yelka, to take another place for herself. Perchets/Steiner was now being protected by several strong-arm Ustacha. His faithful Pospishil was still serving as his chauffeur and all-around protector.

The sybarite still frequented the best nightclubs. He also found himself a new girl friend, an entertainer. Yelka learned of her rival and became jealous enough to desert her lover. Perchets had made a very serious blunder, for Yelka knew too much. When she arrived in Zagreb she was ready to tell all she knew about the Ustacha. For once, the police realized how useful she could be. She was encouraged to write her memoirs, which were published in *Novosti,* one of the capital's more important newspapers. And what a story she had to tell! Yelka exposed the role that Italy and Hungary were playing as instigators of subversion in Yugoslavia. She also revealed how Pavelich and her former lover were living in luxury while their poor deluded followers were being exploited. The scandal ruined Perchets, who disappeared during the summer of 1933 and was never seen again.

6 *Enter Barthou*

The two men who had a rendezvous with death at the hands of the Ustacha on the streets of Marseilles had many interests in common. They were both highly cultured individuals with sensitive natures and a great enthusiasm for rare books. They shared the view that Hitler and Mussolini were determined to rule Europe no matter what the cost.

When the Doumergue Government took power after the downfall of Daladier, Louis Barthou was asked to head the Foreign Office after the post had been turned down by Herriot. At seventy-two, Barthou was still able to put in a long and hard day's work. He generally awoke at five in the morning, took a cold bath, exercised and was shaved by his barber, and then had his breakfast. He was at work at eight o'clock, and he worked through a twelve-hour day.

Barthou loved books, women, and music. He once said that

music was "a means of action which no other art, even the
theatre, possesses to the same degree. A reproduction of a
masterpiece of painting or a sculpture if such is possible is
never the original. It is necessary to go to them. . . . Music
is not a single thing, an inaccessible masterpiece. Everyone
can attempt to realize a perfect interpretation or approach that
perfection. The glories of Beethoven are thereby revealed."

Despite his consistent opposition to German expansionism,
it has been claimed that Louis Barthou never adopted any
rigid position on domestic or foreign affairs. He considered
himself an old-fashioned and rather mild conservative. Yet
one of his colleagues declared, "To have Barthou in one's ministry is a risk, but to have him outside is dangerous." He was
a man who was taken seriously by his political friends and
enemies.

Barthou did have many enemies among the ultra-reaction-
aries in his native land. Daudet, brutal-tongued son of the
famous novelist, who knew that Barthou was a collector of
rare books—some of them on pornography—once wrote that
he patronized brothels every night where he practiced all the
vices of the *Satyricon.*

A widower, Barthou lived with his mother-in-law. He was
not a puritan. He had had a number of affairs with beautiful
women—in a land where such conduct is considered to be
commonplace. Barthou was not the only politician who had
mistresses; most of the country's most eminent men had their
female friends and made no bones about it.

Barthou was a gentle man, but he had a sense of humor and
especially liked to tell bawdy stories. At a party given by a
prominent woman journalist, he told his hostess, in a voice
audible to all, "I have been to bed with every woman at this
table." Then, taking a closer look around, he admitted cheer-
fully, "But that lady over there, sitting between the fat gentleman and the young girl . . . I don't seem to be sure of her."

Barthou's forthright remarks did create some difficult moments for him. On one occasion he received Henri Robert, a member of the Académie Français and the father-in-law of Paul Reynaud, the financial expert who was later to become Premier. "Monsieur," he said, "your name may be illegitimate, but you have made it immortal." The eminent Frenchman was stunned, and never forgave Barthou for that indiscretion.

Experienced journalists, however, praised the Foreign Minister's handling of the press. Of one problem confronting every man in public service, he said: "Since confidential matters are the best form of publicity, I have discovered that there is only one way to keep diplomatic secrets from being printed. I simply tell the newspapermen everything, but at the same time I let them know exactly what things I do not want to make public. And I warn them that whoever breaks my trust will never be received by me."

It was a method that served him well. During his all-too-brief time as his country's Foreign Minister, no state secret of any importance was revealed in the press.

Barthou usually saw the journalists at eight in the morning. His close friend and collaborator Alexis Leger, the permanent official at the Quai d'Orsay, once observed that Barthou was one politician who listened to what other people had to say. "He listens," Leger said, "with a tenseness I have never seen in any other man. He closes his eyes and puts his hands over them. Now and then he interrupts to make one clarify one's words. Finally, he presents you with the gist of the other's statements in an amazingly shrewd and brief synopsis."

During rare moments of relaxation from the cares of his office, he would speculate about the future of Europe to Leger. One day as the two men sat on a bench near the Bois de Boulogne, Barthou talked about the coming tragedy. Profoundly depressed, he observed that a certain dry rot always sets in on men who have been too long in public life. Whatever their hopes and intentions, their creativity is bound to run downhill.

On another occasion he put his hand on Leger's shoulder and said, "We are destined to have a terrible upheaval in France and war is inevitable. Any Frenchman in politics who thinks these things can be avoided is deceiving himself lamentably. Why not face things squarely? Everything has degenerated in France: our perception of the state of public duty in parliament, of our institutions. We have reached the place where we do not know what to do about it all. We cannot act anymore."

At that point he paused, and then declared, "Poor Leger! I am sure if we were to tell each other what lies in our innermost thoughts it would be a pretty dismal tale. I'll tell you frankly though that I think the parliamentary regime is through in France and the nation is lost. . . . I think France is done for."

When Doumergue invited Barthou to become a member of the Cabinet, Europe was at the crossroads. The Nazis hoped to divide the two wartime allies and in the process lull London into the belief that peace was uppermost in Hitler's mind. Barthou readily accepted the post. At last, he must have thought, I will get the Government to pursue a realistic policy toward Germany.

Barthou was one of the very few European statesmen who had read *Mein Kampf,* and he took Hitler's words in that volume as gospel truth—Hitler's truth. Though the experienced Anthony Eden could remark that Hitler was a sincere man with whom it would be possible to come to terms, Barthou insisted that the fanatic was bent on a revanche policy, and not to be trusted.

The Foreign Minister had once remarked to a close friend that he belonged "to the generation of horse sense. I am an old-fashioned Frenchman. I can't help it. All those League of Nations fancies—I would soon put an end to them if I were in power. All this talk about economic sanctions. What does it amount to? It's alliances that count. I would go to different capitals to find out where our friends were, and I would come out into the open with Great Britain and tell her exactly what we ought to do between us to settle the German question."

Britain, of course, was in no mood to listen to Barthou. The British never could understand why he distrusted the Nazis.

Barthou was working against time. He knew that the only effective way of stopping Hitler was to forge a diplomatic ring of iron around the Third Reich. The peace-loving states allied with France would then be able to contain German expansionism even before it had begun to spread. In time the pressure caused by the Allies would force the Junker generals to break with the Hitler regime. But Barthou knew that England and the United States were not aware of the grave danger they faced at the hands of a very hungry and powerful Reich. He despaired about the future of Europe, and feared that the world would be plunged into a frightful war.

Did he see with a prophet's vision what would become of France after Laval took over the Foreign Office portfolio? Did he know that many of France's respected leaders would be acting as their country's gravediggers?

Berlin suddenly made a most enticing offer to the democracies. Hitler said that his Government was willing to cooperate with other states to create a durable peace, and take his nation into the League, if only he was allowed to have an army of 300,000 men.

Barthou had to respond to the German proposal. He knew, of course, that Hitler was only trying to impress the British with his sincerity. As a political realist Barthou knew that one concession made to the Nazis would lead to another and then another. The end of that road would be German control of the entire Continent.

But a number of naive Frenchmen were inclined to trust Hitler. And in Britain, Stanley Baldwin, who had admitted many times that he knew very little about foreign affairs, said that Hitler was justified in asking for more armaments.

Gaston Doumergue and his Cabinet discussed how they
should respond to a Hitler note in which he asked for equality
in arms. Barthou drafted the first reply. The most distinguished
of French statesmen and the army generals were all asked
to study the draft before it was dispatched. Marshal Henri
Philippe Pétain, who was to play so shoddy a role during the
German occupation of France, said that there should be no
compromise with the Nazis. He insisted that there ought be
no disarmament until France was guaranteed her security.
Edouard Herriot, one of the prime movers in the Radical
Socialist Party, and André Tardieu, who had served as an aide
to Georges Clemenceau during the First World War, checked
every word of the draft before it was sent off to Hitler. The
Germans had just released their new budget figures, a cursory
study of which revealed that they were about to rearm at an
alarming rate. Barthou made a thorough study of the budget
and concluded that France had to continue to act from strength
and not compromise her security. He was deeply concerned.
Later, he told Leger he had asked himself: "What would
Aristide Briand have written if he was Foreign Minister?
Would he have made the note strong, or would he have yielded
to Germany in this case, as he did so many times at
Geneva?

"If we refuse Germany's offer, won't Hitler say, 'You see?
We were ready to negotiate, but France refused to accept our
offer. We are in the right, but France sets herself up to be
our judge.'"

He pondered over the note for three days, weighing one
answer against another. Then he discussed the draft with
Leger.

"The essential step," he told his friend, "was the enlarging
of the German war budget. Germany was saying, 'No matter
what happens, I am rearming.' And I say, if we take the fatal
step we shall be forced with new and higher demands in a
short time. One day we shall have to take a stand. It is better

that we take it now while the trump cards are still in our hands."

The "trump cards" were the support the Doumergue Government would receive from the General Staff, the loyalty of the Little Entente, French public opinion, and the participation of Soviet Russia in European affairs as an ally of France.

Barthou gave a luncheon at the Quai d'Orsay on April 16. As the guests were leaving he motioned to Henri Béranger, president of the Foreign Affairs Committee, to remain. Barthou still had some doubts about the final draft of the reply, and he wanted to talk about the matter with his colleague. After listening to him for an hour, Béranger said that the draft met with his approval.

Doumergue looked over the draft the following day. He requested that the Council of Ministers should study it also, and vote for or against the final wording. The meeting of the Council lasted for many hours. By the time agreement had been reached, Barthou was in a state of complete exhaustion. But tired as he was he still wanted to discuss what had happened at the meeting with Leger.

"I was almost alone in the Council of Ministers . . . the only one who stood up for my plan. The Council had drawn up a categorical refusal and this was unanimously adopted. This is a tragic moment for me. Now I must abandon my deepest convictions. I thought of resigning, but then I decided I have no right to do so. As a Minister of the National Union I must sacrifice my personal opinion for the sake of the general good. And now it is the Committee's decision which we must abide by. From now on we shall need great courage and true allies."

Barthou wanted the note to contain a conciliatory tone. He had no intention of appeasing Hitler, but he knew that Britain could interpret a stiff French note as a typical example of Gallic stubbornness. Germany would appear to be the injured party, while France would be placed in the role of a Shylock insisting upon a pound of flesh from her poor abused neighbor. But the Council of Ministers felt that this was no time to play games. The Republic was in danger, and the Reich must be told that there would be no compromise unless Berlin underwent a change of attitude.

France's answer to Germany's note went off on April 17. Barthou was given most of the credit for the final draft. Many knowledgeable politicians expressed their doubts about it. One of the more cynical of the lot said, "I know Barthou. He insists so frantically that it is his note because he had nothing to do with it."

Barthou himself told Campbell, the British Chargé d'Affaires in Paris, "I know perfectly well that our note will cause deep disappointment in the British Cabinet. But when a government contains six ex-Presidents of the Council, five of whom have been Ministers of Foreign Affairs, that government knows what it is doing and one can be assured that it represents the wishes of the French people."

He still believed that European security against aggression could be achieved only with an alliance with Russia. In discussing that issue with Leger he said, "The Right expects me to relieve it of the Russian offer of collaboration. So tell me of all the transactions with the Soviets."

Leger gave Barthou a thorough briefing on past negotiations with the Russians, to which Barthou listened with his customary concentration, his eyes closed. Leger told him about Dovaleski's proposal of a military alliance. Barthou did not think that an alliance would be possible immediately, but would have to wait for future developments. An alliance would conflict with other French arrangements. A security pact, however, might be feasible, he told Leger. "If we did not take advantage of it we would be throwing the Soviets into the arms of the Germans."

"We ought," Leger said, "to mold the Soviet plan into an acceptable shape, including its limitation to Europe, and a provision that the Soviets must join the League of Nations. The Kremlin must understand that France insists that this should be a collective plan, and that the pact will have to be coordinated with the other treaties in which France assumed certain obligations—in other words, that this will be a true collective pact open to Germany as well as Russia. Another Locarno obliges France to assist Russia against Germany, but it also obliges her to assist Germany against Russia. Up to the present our negotiations in this respect have been extremely satisfactory."

Leger discoursed for an hour, whereupon Barthou thanked him for "a brilliant exposition."

Barthou was of light heart when he arrived in London to discuss his new pact with the British. He had let it be known that he preferred to dispense with the usual pageantry accorded a distinguished foreign visitor: there was work to be done. He was confident he would be able to convince Downing Street that the plan would succeed, that if it were adopted it would be an effective means of maintaining the peace and securing the other European nations from aggression.

But his mood took a decided change when the French Ambassador told him that his so-called flirtations with the Russians had irritated his hosts. He encountered a chilly atmosphere when he had his first meeting with the London politicians. One French journalist who accompanied Barthou later wrote: "The French Foreign Minister was treated more like a criminal before a court of justice than as an honored guest."

The talks got under way. It was heartening for Barthou to see a decided change in the British attitude after he had explained what he was trying to accomplish.

"It's wonderful," Vansittart exclaimed. "It does not seem possible. What a victory for collective security! And what a diplomatic victory over the Russians. Here is the justification for Locarno."

After Leger informed the British that France intended to extend the guarantee to Germany and come to her defense if Russia attacked her, Sir John Simon hastened to give his seal of approval to the Barthou pact.

The British Government sent a draft to its ambassadors in Berlin and Warsaw, informing them of what had transpired in London. "Great Britain is wholly in favor of the Barthou pact," went the message, "and her diplomats are instructed to make (it) known in their respective posts."

This was rather reassuring to Barthou. Later events, of course, were to demonstrate that all was not what it appeared to be. The British had not actually been sold on the pact at all.

Barthou was not surprised when he was told that the Germans reacted violently when they heard what had happened at the London meeting. Herr von Ribbentrop, former wine salesman and Hitler's advisor on foreign affairs, came to Paris and insisted on seeing Leger. He was received by the foreign service official, and Leger explained what Barthou was trying to do. Ribbentrop listened. He yawned rudely and stretched his legs, and then he shouted, "That thing, never!"

Leger warned him that "It would be serious if you reject it, for then it will be said that Germany did not want peace to come to Europe." The neophyte diplomat, who had at one time entertained an ambition to become an actor, still insisted that the Reich would have no part of an Eastern Locarno. He yawned once more and then, rising from his chair, repeated his scornful shout: "No, we could never enter an Eastern pact, never!"

This was exactly the kind of response Barthou had expected from the Germans. Hitler was still trying to detach Britain from her tacit alliance with France, hoping to wreck the alliance of the Little Entente with Paris and then isolate the ancient enemy of the Reich. Barthou knew that both Rome and Berlin were trying to get rid of Benes, Titulescu, and King Alexander. As long as those men were alive and in power,

Germany had no chance of winning over the smaller nations and inducing them to join the totalitarian camp.

The three men who stood in the way of the dictators were convinced that Russia would have to be included in any future security pact. While they were no friends of the Communists, they reasoned that ideology ought not to impede a mutual security agreement. They believed that a French-sponsored Eastern Locarno, including the Little Entente, Russia, and the other countries of Southern Europe, would be a powerful bulwark against any military thrust by the Teutons or their Latin partners.

Barthou planned to bring his Eastern Locarno into being in a few months. He had asked Poland to join with her neighbors and become a member of this semi-alliance. There was no doubt that the League of Nations would sanction the pact; nothing in it violated the League's Covenant.

Barthou's concept was nothing new. The Herriot Government had signed a non-aggression pact with Moscow on August 29, 1931. When Maxim Litvinoff came to Paris during July 1933, he was greeted enthusiastically by the people. Pierre Cot, the French Air Minister, had flown to Moscow with an air squadron in the early fall of 1933 and had received a royal welcome from the Russians. Stalin was more than willing to be convinced that an Eastern Locarno was essential to protect his country from a German invasion. His intelligence agents in Europe had reported that Hitler and his Nazi associates were planning to colonize the Soviet Ukraine with German settlers.

On Februay 16, 1933, the foreign ministers of Roumania, Yugoslavia, and Czechoslovakia had affixed their signatures to a document calling for the establishment of a permanent council pledged to act together against any nation seeking to destroy the status quo by force. At their July 1933 meeting, Litvinoff and the French Goverment concluded an agreement defining what constituted aggression.

The Francophile Nicolas Titulescu said that the time was ripe to set up a "Balkan Locarno." At the foreign ministers' meeting in Athens on the very day Barthou became Foreign Minister, an agreement was signed that united the nations against those who were trying to rewrite the Treaty of Versailles by the exercise of force.

A totally unexpected event took place after the Greeks and the Turks signed the pact. Colonel Kimon Georgiev staged a coup and overthrew the totalitarian-oriented regime in Sofia. He changed the pro-German foreign policy of his country and turned it toward the democracies. His first act was to declare the I.M.R.O. illegal. He destroyed the terrorist organization and forced Ivan Mikhailov to flee to Turkey. The new Bulgarian Government signed a treaty of peace with the Yugoslavs on May 24, 1934—an unexpected present for the Little Entente and France.

A Roumanian-Greek-Bulgar rapprochement was consummated during November 1934. The Balkan nations adopted "statutes" modeled after those of the Little Entente. A permanent council and other agencies were brought into being. The new developments clearly indicated that the smaller nations were determined to play an important role in the future. Barthou was gratified. He knew that, given enough time, he would be able to create a grand alliance that would also include the Western Powers.

7 *The Ersatz Caesar*

Though Barthou was aware that Hitler represented a great danger to the peace of Europe, he entertained an illusion that Mussolini could be induced to stand with France against German aggression. He was, of course, mistaken. Mussolini was the first politician to establish a right-wing totalitarian regime on the Continent, and his method of eliminating political enemies was to kill them off. Hitler studied Mussolini's methods, and copied them when he got to power.

The Duce and his Fascisti were installed as the Italian Government by a weak and vacillating monarch in the early 1920s. As soon as Mussolini had been given the power, he announced to the world that Italy would take over Trentino, Gorizia, Trieste, and Western Istria, with or without the consent of her former allies. The territory had been promised before Italy had entered the war on the Allied side. When the new

Kingdom of Yugoslavia was created by the peacemakers at Versailles, Italy was certain she had been swindled by Lloyd George, Wilson, and Clemenceau. Wilson, who had been hailed as a savior by the Italian people and the press, was soon denounced as a turncoat and a hypocrite. Hysterical Italian politicians had led their constituents to believe that Wilson had promised them a vast amount of land, all of which was inhabited by Slavs. It did not matter that Wilson had not actually done any such thing. The newspapers and the postwar Italian leaders still insisted that he had, and continued to slander him.

From the Italian viewpoint, the Versailles Peace Conference was a total disaster. Journalists raved about the "treachery of the perfidious Allies" and moaned about Italy winning the war and losing the peace. The Italian leaders overacted, and the people reflected the attitudes that had been struck by their politicians. In that emotional state of mind they were ready to wage war against anyone who stood in their way. The politicians outdid each other in casting insults at their former allies. Not one responsible leader mentioned what France had done on the battlefields of Flanders, at the Marne and at Verdun, or that despite her great loss of men she had not received everything she had asked for, either. Nor did the Italian politicians tell their people that the French were taking their disappointment in a mature manner.

Borghese, in his study of the Italian character after the First World War, wrote: "An unprecedented miracle of psychopathic alchemy had been performed. Italy, or at least the intellectual and political elite to which an evil destiny has entrusted Italy, had transsubstantiated a victory into a disaster. . . . The nation, masochism-stricken, exulted in frustration."

The hysterical state of mind of the Italians made them vulnerable to the propaganda of the Duce. This man who was to become Europe's first totalitarian ruler had begun the prime phase of his political career as a militant Socialist. He also claimed to be against all wars. Before the French Government bribed him into changing his attitude toward the war, Mussolini had written:

"In time of war the bourgeoisie confronts the proletariat with the tragic dilemma: either insurrection, easily drowned in blood, or cooperation in joint butchery. This second alternative of the dilemma is cloaked under the words fatherland, duty, territorial integrity, etc. Yet the root of the matter never changes. Here is the real reason why we hate war."

The Duce was still very much the Socialist when he scoffed at the plight of the Belgians after their country had been occupied by the German Army. "They ask us to shed tears over the martyrdom of Belgium. This is but a sentimental comedy staged by France and Belgium. These two harridans would like to exploit universal gullibility. To us, Belgium is a belligerent country, no different from all others. It is our right and duty to urge the revolt of the working classes against today's events."

Shortly after he had enlightened his readers about the invasion of Belgium, Mussolini accepted a bribe from the French Government. And during the month of October 1914, he ceased being an anti-imperialist and became an enthusiastic spokesman for the Allied cause.

He suggested that Italy should break with the Central Powers and align herself with France and England. He insulted the Socialists who were still against Italy's participation in the war, calling them "traitors and deserters." With funds the French had given him, he published a new daily newspaper, *Il Popolo d'Italia*. He demanded that the Italian people should mobilize themselves in a "War of Liberation" to save themselves from being a downtrodden race. Socialism, he said, would triumph. The Italians must respect the self-determination of all peoples. The Croats, the Slovenes, the Serbs would all sit down like brothers with their Latin friends after the war had been won.

Looking back into the past, he wrote: "For the last hundred years the Germans have been poisoned by a constant apology of the blond-haired race, the only race capable of creating and propagating Kultur in a decaying Europe. The empire was to be the instrument for this work of salvation. But the empire as it tries to spread is discovering the limitations of power. The empire in trying to dilate dies. History has witnessed the downfall of three empires: the empire of Charlemagne, the empire of Charles V, and the empire of Napoleon. No better fate has been reserved for that fourth empire—the Pope's—in the spiritual domain. It too has crumbled. A like destiny lies in store for the Fifth Empire that has been lured by Wilhelm Hohenzollern in his megalomania. Germany must be crushed. And she can be crushed quickly with the help of Italy. The giant has created a monstrous machine—militarism—to insure its dominion over all peoples. This machine must be smashed. What a historic day it will be when the factories of the pederast Krupp go up in flames that will illuminate all of Europe and purify Germany. In the name of the Belgian towns and cities which have been paralyzed and destroyed, in the name of the numberless victims of this war which was unleashed by bestial German pride, Essen, city of guns and cannons, must be razed to the ground. Only then will the pillaging and murderous Germans reacquire the rights of citizenship in humanity."

Toward the end of the conflict Mussolini ceased being either Socialist or Democrat and became an ultra-nationalistic totalitarian. The former critic of imperialism now demanded that Dalmatia, Fiume, and African colonies were necessary for Italy's survival. The French, Americans, and British, who had been hailed by him as true defenders of democracy, were now called "wolves and jackals" who must be destroyed. He said that the League of Nations was "a sort of monstrous, idealistic plutocratic abortion" and advised the Italians to "invite His Holiness to decamp from Rome and go back to Avignon or, in conformity with the predilections developed by the Vatican during the war, to take up residence among the Boche."

Mussolini was against everyone by this time. "We have torn up all the revealed truths, we have spat on all dogmas, rejected all paradises, scorned all charlatans: the whites (Liberals), the Reds (Socialists) and the Blacks (Catholics). Encyclicals today are issued from two Vaticans: that of Rome and that of Moscow. We are heretics of both these religions."

By 1922 he had established his own religion—Fascism. He took a hard look at England and did not like what he saw. He wrote that "England has practiced the most complete deception possible on Europe and the world. It is from London that the postwar doctrine of reconstruction has emerged. . . . We have never for one moment been taken in by that solemn league of crooks that sits at Geneva oblivious of the ridicule that surrounds it. Nor have we ever believed in English pacifism or English reconstructionism, or in any of the nebulous League theories which are wafted over the Anglo-Saxon world. It is not in Italy's interest to support the British Empire. It is in her interest to contribute to its downfall.

"By hurling the Italians as a single force towards world tasks, by turning the Mediterranean into an Italian lake, by allying ourselves with those who dwell on the Mediterranean and driving out those who are its parasites, by accomplishing this long, arduous, Cyclopean task, we shall truly inaugurate a magnificent era in Italian history."

And assuming the role of a latter-day prophet, he saw a time coming when the territory handed over to Yugoslavia would be forcibly torn away again. "The Dalmatian coast has been betrayed, but it has no intention of accepting surrender."

By the mid-1920s, the former idealist had become a most cynical politician: "Humanity is still and always will be an abstraction of time and space; men are still not brothers, do not want to be, and evidently cannot be. Peace is hence absurd, or rather it is a pause in war. There is something that binds man to his destiny of struggling against his fellows or himself. The motives for the struggle may change indefinitely, they may be economic, religious, political, sentimental, but the legend of Cain and Abel seems to be the inescapable reality, while brotherhood is a fable which men listen to during the bivouac of truce. The Christian and Socialist 'men be brothers' is a mask for the eternal and immutable 'homo homini lupus,' and man will continue to be a wolf among wolves for a bit of land, for a trickle of water, for a crumb of bread, for a necessity or a caprice; he will continue to ignore others and ignore himself."

The evolution of Benito Mussolini from a semi-pacifist-Socialist to a warlike dictator was wondrous to behold. A year after the Locarno Pact had been signed, calling for the countries of Europe to keep the peace and come to the aid of nations attacked by an aggressor, Mussolini forced a pact of his own down the throats of the Albanians, supposedly to protect the mountain people from their enemies. The enemy, as defined by Mussolini, was Yugoslavia. In effect, the new pact transformed Albania into an Italian satellite. Mussolini now had a base from which his army could mount an attack on the Yugoslavs. In his mind it was only a matter of time before the Italians would sweep into Yugoslavia and take over the country.

French politicians including Barthou still believed that Italy's vital interests called for an alliance with France. They also thought that blood was thicker than ideology. But for years the Duce had been helping the I.M.R.O. and giving funds to the Ustacha. Both organizations he considered his spearheads—in a manner of speaking his assault troops in the Balkans. Mussolini was motivated by an idée fixe—he wanted to revive the ancient Roman Imperium. In the end, he became an ardent and enthusiastic ally of Hitler.

8 The East Europeans

While Louis Barthou was still thinking about going to Rome to talk to Mussolini about a Mediterranean Pact, he became increasingly disturbed by the strange behavior of the Polish leader, Marshal Pilsudski. The grizzled old militarist was showing signs of getting ready to divorce France and join up with the Germans.

Marshal Pilsudski was a dreamer. He had begun his political career—if it could be called that—as a member of a Nihilist-Anarchist organization called Bojowa. Polish Socialists called Bojowa "Le Club des Assassins." As the acknowledged leader of these terrorists, Pilsudski led a band that held up a Czarist Government train loaded with bullion. He organized the Polish Legion that fought with the Germans against the Russians at the Battle of Tannenberg. The Prussians, arrogant as usual, did not treat the proud Pole with the deference he felt should be accorded him. He rebelled against them and was put into prison.

Pilsudski spent the last few months of World War I in the military fortress at Magdeburg, and was released only after the Armistice had been declared. The Allies distrusted him, as well they should have. Poland was not represented by the flamboyant Marshal at Versailles. The Big Three indicated that they preferred doing business with Ignace Paderewski, the pianist turned statesman, and Roman Dmowski. Both men had been pro-Ally during the war.

No sooner was Poland established than her leaders ordered her army to invade Russia. General Haller's legions reached the gates of Kiev before they were thrown back in disorder. The soldiers did not stop running until they had reached the gates of Warsaw. At that moment of crisis, French generals took over the defense of the embattled city. Pilsudski was there to advise the military. The Russian Army was defeated and forced to retreat; Pilsudski was thereupon regarded as a great hero by his easily impressed countrymen.

The ex-anarchist and ex-train robber, who had considered himself a Socialist of sorts in the far distant past, now became a fanatic nationalist. Holding Paderewski in complete contempt, in time he staged a coup and overthrew the democratic government in Warsaw. His first act was to order the Sejm (the Polish parliament) dissolved—spelling the doom of the infant Polish democracy. His second act was to promote himself to the rank of a Marshal of Poland.

Pilsudski ruled a nation in which feudal aristocrats controlled most of the economy. He resented Poland's dependence on France for her security. Though he admired Hitler's daring, he was well aware that the Reich was a danger to peace. He proposed that France, Poland, and the Little Entente should wage a preventive war against Germany. When the French refused to go along with this suggestion, he decided that the time had come for him to change his foreign policy and reach an understanding with the Führer.

The Marshal entertained a healthy admiration for the powers of the German Army. To Gustav Stresemann, when they met in Geneva, he said, "It was a glorious army, the old German Army. I always had a great deal of respect for the German Army." Pilsudski had no notion that the Polish chicken would be devoured in a few gulps by the hungry German wolf.

A lesser Romantic would have known that the wolf's first bite would be the Polish Corridor and the Free City of Danzig. Hitler had said as much in *Mein Kampf*. But Pilsudski was apparently convinced that the ravenous beast was about to become quite tame. The old Marshal had practically made up his mind to pry his country loose from her ancient friend, France, when Barthou left Paris for Warsaw.

By that time, Germany and Japan were no longer members of the League of Nations. The Japanese Army had run amok in China and had established a puppet regime in Manchuria. Other Chinese provinces had been invaded, and there was no telling where Japan would stop. Japanese aggression in Asia was forcing the Russians to re-examine their foreign policy. They knew that their western border would have to be secured against an attack by the Germans. Since no one knew when the Japanese might crash into Siberia, the possibility of a two-front war was giving Stalin many a sleepless night.

The Russian dictator had no illusions about Hitler. If he ever had had any, they were quickly dispelled when Alfred Hugenberg, former Chairman of the Nationalist Party and at that time Reich Minister of Economics and Agriculture, delivered a badly timed speech at the London Economic Conference. In typical Teutonic fashion he demanded that Germany be given a mandate to use her "constructive and creative genius to reorganize Russia."

After that, Herbert Dirksen, the German Ambassador to Moscow, informed his Government that Stalin had decided he had better "step over to a safer atmosphere of Anglo-French collaboration."

By revealing the true intentions of the Reich, Hugenberg

had flung egg onto Germany's face. Hitler shared the man's ideas about the future of Russia, but he hardly wanted his plans disclosed to the world at such an early date. He removed Hugenberg from office. But the damage had been done. Stalin was now more determined than ever to mend his fences in Western Europe. Time was running out for his country.

Barthou knew Russia was afraid of a two-front war. He concluded that Stalin really had no choice: he had to join up with France and her allies and agree to go along with Barthou's concept of an Eastern Locarno.

The Frenchman expected to encounter some difficulties when he broached the subject to the Roumanians and the Yugoslavs. They were afraid of Russia and did not trust her. But he was sure that he would be able to convince them that their future security rested on a pact that would include the USSR.

Roumania had helped herself to the province of Bessarabia after the First World War, and had no intention of giving it back. Alexander of Yugoslavia did not relish the idea of becoming an ally of a regime that had ordered the killing of the Romanoff family. But he was a sensible man and would, Barthou anticipated, agree that an Eastern Locarno without Russia would be a weak reed if and when the Germans invaded the Balkans.

Actually, the Balkans had been liberated by the Russian Army. Troops of the Czar had defeated the Turks and finally ended their century-old control over the peninsula. Many South Slavs regarded Russia as their big brother of the North. Blood, they felt, would tell in the end even though Russia was ruled by the Communists.

Barthou, who never took any ideology seriously, always believed that Russia and France were natural allies. They had been linked ever since the days when the first Napoleon and his Grand Armée had been destroyed on Russia's icy steppes.

France had learned much since that time, and would always look to the East for help if the Teuton went on a rampage.

By the early 1930s, the Moscow Government had become more acceptable to France and her friends. On January 25, 1932, Litvinoff signed a non-aggression pact with Poland. On November 29 of that year a similar agreement was arrived at with France. Moscow had also reached an understanding with Finland, Estonia, and Latvia. During July and August of 1932, the Kremlin established normal diplomatic relations with China. And on July 17, 1933, the Russian Government was recognized by the United States, with an exchange of ambassadors.

Russia, much as Barthou had appraised the situation, was being forced to meet the West halfway. She was in need of a concord with France, Litvinoff admitted to William Bullitt when asked what had caused the change in his country's foreign policy. The little diplomat told Bullitt that an agreement with Paris was important because the Soviet Union had valid reason to suspect Japan was planning to invade Siberia in the spring.

Moscow, according to Litvinoff, did not think that Poland and Germany would attack in the immediate future. If the Japanese-Russian war lasted for two years, Germany and Poland would attack Russia from the west. The Kremlin, Litvinoff said, knew all about the preliminary talks that had taken place between Japan, Germany, and Poland. Russia knew that the three powers had arrived at an agreement on when an invasion should take place.

Litvinoff also explained to Bullitt that Russia did not have much faith in the effectiveness of the League of Nations. His Government had decided to become a member of that body at the urging of France. It was a price the Kremlin was prepared to pay for Gallic friendship.

9 Pilsudski

Poland's relations with Germany had never been too friendly. The Germans had suffered from a compulsion to march to the east, ever since the days when Teutonic knights had staged their forays into lands inhabited by Slavs centuries ago. Germany had been in on the partition of Poland, along with the Russians and the Austrians, and now they were at it again. Hitler was fulminating about the Corridor and Danzig, telling his people that the territory was German, had always been German, and someday would be German once more.

Pilsudski did not attribute any importance to Hitler's warlike statements. He said the Führer was simply trying to keep his followers happy with some inexpensive demagoguery. The Marshal gave most of his attention to the Russians, for whom he nursed a deep hatred. He grumbled also that the French had always relegated Poland to a very minor role in European affairs, never appreciating his country, and failing to understand what he, Pilsudski, was trying to achieve. Poland, he said, must be restored to her ancient grandeur.

The dictator in the Belvedere Palace was becoming more and more suspicious of his French ally. Joseph Paul Boncour, while serving as French Foreign Minister, had been one of the sponsors of a Four-Power Pact. Pilsudski suspected that this Pact included some secret clauses calling for Poland to give up part of her real estate to Germany.

Barthou had no intention of forcing Poland to give up anything to Germany. He told his colleagues that Pilsudski's foreign policy was fraught with danger for both France and Poland. He knew enough about the Polish leader and the Polish character to believe that excessive pride could lead them all into very perilous international waters.

France had been instrumental in winning freedom for Poland: Georges Clemenceau at Versailles was mainly responsible for bringing Poland back to life. And it was General Weygand and his staff who helped the Poles when the Russian Army invaded their country. But Pilsudski preferred to forget what France had done. By some kind of twisted logic he concluded that Poland would only achieve greatness if she turned her back on France and everything French. Lust for Poland's recognition as one of Europe's major powers was causing Pilsudski to move toward the German camp.

The Marshal's dream of power and grandeur was based on self-delusion. His country's total population was thirty million. Eight million were Ukrainians, Jews, and White Russians. The Ukrainians had revolted against Polish rule during the 1920s; they still nursed a deep feeling of resentment against their overlords. The Jews certainly had no reason to feel loyal to the state: they were a sorely persecuted minority. The economy was agrarian, the industrial base almost non-existent. Any ruler should have known that a nation with a backward economy and ill-digested minorities numbering in the millions was

hardly in a position to play the role of a great power. But
Pilsudski and his countrymen thought hope was the father
of reality. Courage, in their lexicon, was equivalent to victory
in time of war. That belief led to their use of cavalry to stop
Panzer divisions during the Second World War.

Hitler was more than willing to promise Pilsudski anything
if it would lure him into the Nazi camp. On May 9, 1933, he
told Alfred Wysocki, the Polish Ambassador to Berlin, that
he wanted to establish friendly relations between the two
countries. The question of the Polish Corridor presented some
difficulties, to be sure, but Hitler hastened to say that men of
good will would be able to resolve them. He, for one, wanted
to see a warm friendship arising. He hoped that Pilsudski
would indicate that Poland was ready to come to terms with
the Reich.

Pilsudski did not react immediately to Hitler's offer of
friendship, but the Führer bided his time. By May 15 when
Joseph Lipski, the new Polish Ambassador, arrived in the
German capital, Warsaw and Berlin had issued a joint com-
munique stating that "all questions affecting the two countries
should be dealt with by way of direct negotiations," and furthermore, that in the interests of peace in Europe "both countries should renounce all use of force in their reciprocal relations."

There was no mention of renouncing war as an instrument
of politics, nor was there any assurance from either of the
two leaders that other nations would be spared from their aggressive designs. Peace was not, of course, the motivating
force as far as the two leaders were concerned. They were
not thinking of keeping the peace. They were bent on waging
war against Russia and the Little Entente.

On November 22, von Moltke, who was serving as the German Ambassador in Warsaw, submitted an offer for a non-
aggression pact to Pilsudski. Shortly thereafter, the Polish Government announced that it had agreed with Germany on a

ten-year non-aggression pact. The Western democracies were shocked when the news was released. Hitler had in one maneuver upset the postwar balance of power on the Continent.

On that same November day in 1933, the French newspaper *Le Matin* disclosed that Hitler had offered a non-aggression pact to the Czechs, and that Benes had turned it down. The Czech leader advised all interested governments that he had no intention of deserting the French camp.

"I rejected this proposal and immediately informed Paris, London, Warsaw, Belgrade and Bucharest of the situation," he said. Unlike his Polish neighbor, Benes never had any illusions about Hitler.

When Barthou was about to undertake his trip to Eastern Europe, he told Leger that Pilsudski was now asking for a permanent seat on the League of Nations Council. Representatives of the major powers were the only diplomats ever chosen for that distinction. When Barthou met with Pilsudski at the Belvedere Palace on April 26, 1934, he found the Pole in an agitated frame of mind. *Kurjer Poranny* reported that Barthou had made a valiant attempt to reason with the Marshal.

"I think," he had said, "that so great a power as Poland ought to have a permanent seat on the Council."

Hearing what he thought was a hint of sarcasm, Pilsudski appeared to be offended. He had replied, "Perhaps you don't desire to cede, but in this case it will become necessary for you to resign or the Chamber will vote against you and your Cabinet will fall. Do you recall our visit to Verdun? You tripped in crossing a field which had been ploughed with artillery shells. Someone came to your aid, but you said that it was useless, that you were in the habit of falling already over twelve times as a Cabinet minister."

"We will continue the same politics in France to secure the peace," Barthou had said in a calm voice, pretending that he had not heard the remark.

"Can you continue it if Germany is against it? You won't be able to," Pilsudski had insisted.

The Marshal was very angry because France had decided to align herself with the Soviets. Barthou was in Warsaw to see for himself how Pilsudski would react to the step he had taken. He knew that Colonel Beck, Pilsudski's foreign relations expert, had always favored a rapprochement with Germany, and had been in large measure responsible for the ten-year pact that had startled the world.

Just before departing Paris, Barthou told a French news-paperwoman that he was "afraid the gentlemen in Warsaw like the Germans better than they do the Russians. I shall be harsh with Pilsudski on the subject of an Eastern Locarno, and yet I am worried about his reactions."

The journalist, who was worried also, told Barthou that she had been in Berlin when the non-aggression pact was signed, and had had an interview with Count Lipski, who had said, "Poland has no need of France from now on, and she is sorry now she ever accepted French aid because of the price she'll have to pay for it." An Eastern Locarno was "out of the question now," Lipski had continued, because "it would be an admission of weakness to Moscow."

Barthou approached Warsaw in some trepidation. His arrival was marred by a display of petty ill-nature on the part of Colonel Beck, who ordered Barthou's train sidetracked to an out-of-the-way railroad station a few miles from the capital. Beck knew that the Polish people would give the Frenchman a warm welcome, but he was determined that Barthou should come into the city like a thief in the night.

Barthou himself described his entry into Warsaw: "We not only arrived without any welcoming ceremony, but we had to carry our own bags, and had difficulty finding taxis."

Colonel Beck (who was an intimate friend of Hermann Goering; they frequently went on boar hunts together) and his attractive wife received Barthou at the Raezynski Palace on the night of his arrival. The Frenchman was tremendously impressed with the feudal splendor of the palace and the "magnificent Polish women and their wonderful jewels—their immense charm and culture. These are the women who have maintained Polish culture through the ages," he said. "What wonderful creatures they are. Why, they know French literature better than I do myself. It is because of that that there still is a Poland."

As expected, Beck greeted Barthou with icy disdain. But the jovial Gaul was able to thaw him out before the evening was over. He drank Polish vodka and praised its quality, and he told Madame Beck that Poland was "one of the greatest facts of contemporary Europe . . . a great and independent nation." Music to the ears of Colonel Beck and his sycophants! Beck decided he would accompany Barthou to the historic city of Cracow.

The Foreign Minister was entranced with the city of famous libraries. Laroche, who was with him on the journey, wrote that Colonel Beck expressed his admiration of Barthou and took note of "his high hat high on his forehead with his jovial air, (his) very youthful allure which did not lack for natural elegance . . . he let himself go with a cordial abandon giving a slight impression of being on a vacation."

But when Barthou asked Beck how he felt about Russia being invited to become a signatory of an Eastern Locarno pact, the Colonel exclaimed, "I haven't enough words to describe my hatred of that country." And after a brief pause he declared, "France needs Poland and not the other way around."

Before Barthou could respond to that non sequitur, Beck delivered a lengthy discourse in which he took both France and Russia to task. The foreign relations expert could not be persuaded that Germany and not Russia was a dangerous ally to have. Beck would have none of that kind of attitude from anyone, least of all Barthou.

The *Petit Parisian*, an important newspaper, had managed

to get hold of a secret document that the Nazi regime had sent to its agents in North and South America. It revealed what Germany had in store for Poland in particular and for Europe as a whole:

"Towards Poland, the National Socialist Government has for the time adopted a more conciliatory attitude, for the reason that on this side special efforts are being made to obtain satisfaction of German claims in another way. Naturally, these claims have by no means been relinquished, any more than the demand for restoration of at any rate a portion of the German overseas colonies. The ultimate aim of the National Socialist regime's foreign policy must be the recovery of all portions of territory around Germany which contain a German minority."

But Colonel Beck, the admirer of Germany, and the ailing Pilsudski—whose mental faculties had been impaired somewhat by his illness—would not or could not see that they were playing with fire. Beck was too busy berating France to stop and consider where Poland's new policies were leading her. His Francophobia had its beginnings when he was Poland's military attaché in Paris in 1921.

Beck had previously been assigned as a military attaché in Prague, where Thomas Masaryk warned the French that Beck was a very dangerous man. The Deuxième Bureau of the War Department had one of its agents contact Beck, posing as an Italian intelligence officer. The "Italian" offered Beck a large sum of money to supply his government with French defense secrets. The Bureau had made arrangements to have Beck lay his hands on a number of faked documents, and Beck sold them to the plant. Paris asked Warsaw to recall Beck, but for some reason never revealed why he was declared persona non grata. General Sikorski, president of the Polish Council, was never informed of what had happened. He was told instead that Beck appeared to be too addicted to wine-women-and-song and was considered an unreliable person.

Beck's pro-German proclivities flowed readily from this demand for his recall. He was a very vindictive man, and now, years later, he was venting his spleen on Barthou especially and the French in general.

A few days after the Beck diatribe, Barthou told a journalist that France "must go ahead with the Locarno of the East. We will count on Russia and not bother anymore about Poland. The Poles are a temperamental people. If they go over entirely to the Germans, so much the worse for them, but I doubt if they would ever do it. What we must do is to win the other nations to the idea and Poland will follow along. Russia must be got to join the League as soon as possible. Before that takes place, however, I shall see that all our little allies of Central Europe are prepared to depend on Russia. I shall visit them to reassure them and I shall say to them, 'I am with you through thick and thin.'"

Before Barthou left Warsaw, Pilsudski told him that the crisis in Europe was caused by the lack of stability of the French Government, and the unrealistic conduct of the great powers at the League of Nations. He said that the League was concentrating too much on trivial problems like white slavery and the opium traffic, and not paying enough attention to reform within the organization. He again insisted that Poland should be awarded a permanent seat on the Council.

Barthou promised Pilsudski that a French military mission would come to Warsaw to discuss mutual military problems. Pilsudski was affronted when the mission arrived a few weeks later led by General Patin, who was serving as his country's military attaché in Bucharest. Pilsudski had expected that a Marshal of France would head the mission.

Kurjer Poranny, in bidding farewell to Barthou, called him "the personification of the magnificent faculties of this land where one sees the spirit of progress allied to the act of patriotism—patriotism to the human idea, respect for traditions with the aspirations of modern democracy."

Thousands of Polish citizens had broken through police cordons set up on the streets of Warsaw and Cracow in order to defy Beck and express their love of France and their respect for Barthou. Even the *Berliner Tageblatt* had some kind words to say about the French Foreign Minister. In Hitler's capital a journalist dared to write: "One sees every day men served by their youth, but it is a rare spectacle to see a man served by his age in order to obtain diplomatic success. What would his visit have been if Barthou was forty!"

If he had failed to impress Pilsudski and Beck, Barthou had won the regard of the people and the newspapermen, and that in itself was an accomplishment of sorts.

When Barthou was asked by reporters whether he considered his trip to Poland a success, he said, "Though Warsaw was not a complete success, the trip can be regarded as a success to a certain extent. The situation had to be clarified. The opposition has become weaker and some misunderstandings have been eliminated. Negotiations on the adjustment of military treaties have been arranged in accordance with the present situation. It seems that Warsaw's opinion on the weakening and the decay of France is changing gradually. France promises for the future to act more in harmony with Warsaw on important questions."

Barthou was not quite as candid as he should have been. Nothing had been settled in Warsaw. How could it have been, when Pilsudski and Beck kept insisting that a war with Russia was inevitable? The two Poles urged Latvia and Estonia to turn down Barthou's proposal that they join an Eastern Locarno. Beck had even made a special trip to both countries and endeavored to make them change their minds. The Polish Government refused to accept any obligation to defend the Czechs if the Germans attacked them. Pilsudski refused to fight the Germans if they invaded Lithuania. The old Marshal was born in that land and hoped to force it into a union with Poland.

It was clear that Poland would not fight the Germans no matter what country they attacked. Neutrality was to be her policy. The two leaders believed that this attitude would somehow tend to deflect Germany away from Polish targets. Pilsudski and Beck considered themselves very brilliant political strategists. They could not perceive that their plans were based on hatred of Russia and jealousy of France, and that in the end their country would be the first to pay the price for their shortsighted behavior toward their former allies.

Barthou left Poland with the knowledge that the old friendship between his country and the nation between the Baltic and the Carpathians was hanging on a thread of frayed silk.

10 Advertising the Idea

The next stop on Barthou's journey was Prague. Czechoslovakia was not Poland. Thomas Masaryk, the father of his country, was a dedicated democrat, and a good friend of France. The President expressed his amazement "at the complete spontaneity, the lack of pretension and the tremendous demonstrations" on the part of the people when they saw Barthou on the streets of their old baroque city.

His greeting included the observation, "The visit of Barthou among us has once more vividly called attention to the numerous ties which unite us to the great French republic. These ties permit us to resist early any chance of crisis and to rise above it with the rest of Europe."

To which Barthou replied: "I wish above all to thank you for this fidelity which is in my eyes your most noble quality, and I add that France returns this to you from her heart and mind. Between our lands there is more than friendship, even more than an alliance, there is true fraternity."

Both men meant what they said; their remarks were not the usual palaver of politicians. The friendship that existed between the French and Czech people was based on a mutual love for freedom and democracy. It took a Daladier to betray that friendship in later years.

Roumania, too, received Barthou with great enthusiasm. He aroused the people to a fever pitch with a speech he delivered in the parliament.

"I am a nationalist, furthermore, because I am ready in every circumstance to give my support without reservation to nations menaced by oppression." He paused to point an accusing finger at Professor Couza, a notorious anti-Semite, and said, "I have never encroached on the liberty of thought and the belief of anyone, and this is what a Christian must do."

The deputies roared their approval when he declared, "If a single centimeter of (Roumanian) territory is touched, France will be at your side. France is with you heart and soul. The use of the word revision in respect to Roumania's unity and her natural frontiers of today would be intolerable treachery. No Roumanian citizen could be a traitor nor could he renounce his rights. We all stand for peace and the well-earned rights that are furnished us."

During the speech, the German and Hungarian ambassadors walked out of the parliament hall in a huff.

After meeting in private with the Roumanian leaders, Barthou set out for Yugoslavia. A train took him to the bank of the Danube River. From that point he traveled on a boat provided by the Yugoslav Government.

M. Pourish of the Foreign Office was there to receive him when he boarded the vessel. Pourish told Barthou that there were Nazi sympathizers high up in his Government. He also said that certain individuals were trying to bring Yugoslavia into the German orbit. Pourish was really revealing his own preferences to Barthou, and the Frenchman knew it.

The boat moved at a leisurely pace along the river toward Belgrade. Serbian cavalrymen raced their horses along the bank and fired their rifles into the air. Barthou stepped ashore at one village to receive the plaudits of the peasants. Pretty girls in colorful native costume sang folk songs and gave him huge bouquets of flowers. One young woman, slightly over-weight, caught his roving eye. Always partial to a pretty woman, he kissed her.

"What a lovely girl," he remarked, "but I am afraid she is a little bit pregnant."

Local musicians played the *Marseillaise* on their native instruments. The mayor of the town made him an honorary citizen, giving Barthou the traditional wine and salt to indicate that he was a well-loved guest. The old Frenchman was pro-foundly moved.

The King awaited him in Belgrade; a session of the Skupsh-tina had been called. The deputies, in native costume, accorded Barthou a boisterous welcome. After he had delivered a speech, he was taken to the Kalemegdan Garden to look at a Mes-trovich sculpture symbolizing French heroism at Salonika, and to the tomb of Serbia's unknown soldier, on a mountaintop about ten miles from Belgrade.

Barthou had a very high regard for the people of this land. He knew that Alexander was a true friend of France. But despite his affection for the Yugoslavs he could not enjoy him-self in their capital. There was very little to be seen there to interest a man like Barthou. Belgrade's night life was dull; the wailings of the gypsy singers bored him. There were no interesting buildings to be examined. The country was wild and primitive, and the capital at that time reflected it. Warsaw may have been unfriendly, but the city was one of the most magnificent in Europe. Cracow was hoary with age and rich in tradition. Bucharest was the little Paris of Eastern Europe, and Prague was a city of unexcelled beauty. The people of

Belgrade were warm enough, but what could a man of discerning tastes find to do there? The palace had rare books, but a man couldn't look through them all the time, after he had had his meeting with the King.

The monotony was broken for a few hours when he was the King's guest at a luncheon in the Dedinje Palace. Prince Paul, the Yugoslav Ambassador to Paris, and other prominent figures were there. Barthou asked the King to visit France. Alexander was reluctant until Barthou gave his personal assurance that he would guide the monarch through the city. Alexander spoke of going to a certain Parisian bookseller to buy some rare books.

"I have long wished to visit this bookshop," he said. "I think the proprietor has something I want, but I cannot be sure from the description he sent me." Barthou, an enthusiastic collector himself, was pleased that he had scored a diplomatic success. The Frenchman did not realize that Alexander had only consented because he wanted to see his oculist in Lausanne; his eyes had been troubling him for some time.

Whatever the King's reasons, the cause of peace would be served by his visit. Barthou took Alexander into his confidence, explaining that he would be going to London to discuss his Eastern Locarno pact with the British. Official England, he sighed, wanted no part of any pact aimed at stopping the Third Reich from its designs. Some of the prominent men in the Government actually suspected that France was about to wage war against Germany.

Barthou also told Alexander that he would be going to Rome in the near future to try to convince the Duce that Germany was the enemy to be feared. Rome, he said, would be asked to become a signatory of a pact which would protect Southern Europe from aggression.

The King was not convinced that Mussolini could be converted into a peace-loving dictator. He told Barthou that Italy was as much a revisionist nation as Hungary and Germany, and that none of the three countries ought to be trusted.

Barthou was well aware that the King and Mussolini made no secret of their dislike for each other. Mussolini had ordered his journalistic mouthpieces to ridicule the King and the Yugoslav nation at every opportunity. Alexander in turn had told *his* journalists to print some embarrassing truths about the Duce and the Italians in general. During September 1934, *San Marco,* an Italian newspaper, publicized the catastrophic Slav defeat at the hands of the Turks at Kosovo, leading to the enslavement of the Slavs by the Turks. Insulting the heroic dead of Kosovo was tantamount to sacrilege as far as the Serbs were concerned. Alexander had reacted violently. The Belgrade paper *Vreme* printed a detailed description of the Italian Army's defeat at Caporetto during the First World War. It was said that the King had written the story himself. The well-known writer Dascalovich also published a book about the Caporetto disaster, depicting the Italian soldiers as a panic-stricken mob who ran away from the Austrians instead of standing up like men and fighting it out with them. The book was placed in all the libraries in the country.

The Italian Ambassador in Belgrade had lodged a protest on behalf of his Government, and demanded that the book be removed from the library shelves. It was finally withdrawn after the Duce promised to stop slandering the Yugoslavs. When, as expected, the Italian newspapers resumed publishing insults about the King and his country, the book was replaced in the libraries.

The quarrel between the King and Mussolini was both personal and political in motivation. The mutual name-calling had been going on for years. The hatred between the two could not be eradicated. The King told Barthou that though Rome would never stop its intrigues against his country, the Duce could never frighten him. He had no intention of giving up an inch of his territory to the Italian dictator. Barthou left Belgrade reassured.

Many months passed. The King's impending visit to France was supposed to be a state secret, but everyone seemed to know about it. There were many talkative politicians in Belgrade, who appeared to delight in telling everyone within earshot that the King was expected to be in Marseilles on October 9. The Italians learned about it and told their hired assassins to get ready. The state visit would present them with an excellent opportunity to kill the King.

Barthou was well pleased with the results of his trip. He had, he felt, convinced the leaders of the Little Entente that France was embarked on a policy which she would maintain even if there was a change in government. France, he had said to them, would always honor her commitments.

But before the old man could relax from his arduous labors, an event occurred that shook the balance of power in Europe to its very foundations. The Austrian Chancellor, Engelbert Dollfuss, was murdered by his own countrymen.

"We are all responsible for Austria," Barthou said when he heard the news. And then emotion got the better of him as he continued, "Little Dollfuss was the very symbol of the fight against Hitler."

Dollfuss, of course, was hardly a symbol for the European democrats. It was he who had ordered the army to attack the Social Democratic workers in his capital. Hundreds of men and women had been killed by the Heimwehr.

Barthou was just completing his eulogy of Dollfuss when Boncour walked into his office. Boncour insisted, "Dollfuss brought this on himself. He juggled with the legitimate maneuvers of Major Fey and Prince Starhemberg's ambitions, with the result that he cut the ties between himself and the Austrian people. Believe me," Boncour told Barthou, "you cannot suppress the Socialist parties in a country without having a collapse. If there is anything left of what in the nineteenth century was called Europe, then this international gangsterism must be stopped."

Barthou had to agree. But how, he asked, was the gangsterism to be ended? Mussolini had been the first to practice politics by terror. The Socialist Matteotti had been gunned down by the Duce's henchmen in 1923. He had ordered the murder of the Roselli brothers in France. Now he was plotting to do away with Alexander. Hitler, imitating Mussolini, had directed the June 30, 1934, bloodbath of his own followers.

Barthou knew the Nazis had marked him as their next victim. But he was not ready to acknowledge that Mussolini's agents would also like to see him out of the way. Any criticism of Louis Barthou would have to be based on his faith that the Duce was a civilized ruler; that faith was his single biggest mistake.

Richard von Koestler, who did not like the Nazis but who had been Germany's Ambassador to Paris before the establishment of the dictatorship and was still serving his country during the first Hitler years, had earlier confided to a friend that Berlin had compiled a list of foreign leaders whom it planned to have executed.

"If you only knew what they are talking about in Germany! A few more assassinations like this one [referring to the murder of Premier Duca by the Roumanian Iron Guard] and Germany will be able to solve her problems and reach her goal without resorting to war in Europe."

His friend interrupted him: "That is nothing new in the life of the Weimar Republic."

"Yes," von Koestler replied, "but the results of which I speak are expected from murders in other countries, not our own. They claim that Germany can affect the economy of war with six judicious political assassinations.

"First there will be Dollfuss. According to Berlin he is the only Austrian who is in serious opposition to the Anschluss. Berlin believes that the partisans of Anschluss are increasing in Austria, and [the Reich] counts on his own countrymen to draw away from Dollfuss. After him, the King of Yugoslavia. Berlin believes that with him out of the way there will be no chance of a political alliance between Yugoslavia and France.

Then they want to do away with Titulescu, who is in the good graces of London and Paris."

"Do you think they had anything to do with the assassination of Duca?" the friend asked.

"Perhaps. I really don't know," von Koestler replied.

It was well known that the Iron Guard, a pro-Fascist organization in Roumania, was being subsidized by Berlin and to some extent by Rome. Just before he was murdered, Duca had told a close friend that the Iron Guard was receiving funds from Germany and Italy.

Von Koestler resumed his recitation. "Then they want to liquidate Benes. Once this has been done they hope the German minority in Czechoslovakia will come running into the arms of Berlin."

"That makes four. Are there any more on the death list?" his friend asked.

"Well, there is Albert, King of the Belgians. Albert has been a traditional enemy in German eyes. At the Wilhelmstrasse they think that as long as Albert lives, Belgium will never enter the German system."

A few months later, von Koestler died in the American Hospital in Paris, shortly after his return there. Hitler had invited him to Berlin for a briefing. After a long discussion, the Führer was not pleased with his Ambassador. Von Koestler had been in good health up to the time of his last interview with Hitler.

11 Killers for Hire

After a few years of totalitarian dictatorships on the Continent a professional killer was considered to be almost a respectable man. When the three Ustacha killers were caught before they were able to assassinate Alexander in Sofia, the Italian press praised them as "heroes."

Twelve days after that unsuccessful episode, the Iron Guard murdered Duca. The Italian newspapers glorified the murderers. The very respectable *Corriere della Sera* of Milan, regarded today as one of the more responsible journals in Italy, said of the untimely demise of the Roumanian Premier that regret over the murder "could not and should not prevent one from realizing the essentially political significance of that kind of violence." The paper's editorialists attributed the murder to the pro-French policies adopted by the "restless and ambitious Titulescu."

The readers of the highly regarded paper were also told that

Getting into the car . . .

Barthou and Alexander . . .

The crowd just after the shot . . .

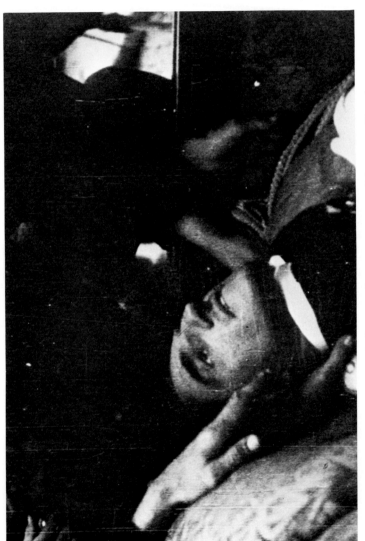

The dead king. (All photographs courtesy Hearst Metrotone News)

"The Iron Guard represents, whether one likes it or not, a new energy which is trying to assert itself outside the customary parliamentary combines. If the Draconian provisions adopted against this organization exasperated its members and provoked the crime, responsibility redounds on those who adopted those ill-advised measures of repression. It is hoped that the Roumanian people will provide themselves with a truly modern regime which will be independent in international affairs."

In other words, if a government was pro-French, its leaders should be liquidated.

Turin Stampa, a periodical oriented toward the Right, expressed its opinions more bluntly: "Roumania desired to cut loose from France and the League of Nations which was under French domination." It accused Duca of being a puppet of France, and said that the Bucharest Government's foreign policy was controlled by Paris, which it blamed for ordering the Roumanian leaders to put "an end to philo-Fascist and philo-Hitlerian agitation."

There were no lengths to which the controlled Italian press would not go to glorify the assassins. *Il Solco Fascista*, an official organ of the Fascist Party in Reggio Emilia, was amused at the precautionary measures being taken by the Roumanian police to assure the safety of Titulescu.

"Who knows," one of the writers asked, when "some students might resort to a rash act."

This was practically inviting a Roumanian Fascist to kill Titulescu.

In an article which was not bylined, a Fascist writer stated that the French could learn from his Party about proper attitudes toward violence. Fascists approved of violence, he said, and the totalitarian philosophy tended to make the "people . . . rise to greater heights" and instilled in them "the feeling of their own independence, pride of nationality and (a) concept of the authoritarian state."

When Oreb and his fellow assassins were tried in Zagreb for the attempted murder of King Alexander, the *Gazzetta del Popolo* said that "no one could check the ulterior developments of the Croat struggle against Belgrade."

The *Corriere della Sera* never mentioned that Oreb and his fellow Ustacha had received most of their training in the arts of murder in Italy. The *Giornale d'Italia* published a Hungarian journalist's interview with Ante Pavelich. The article clearly stated that Pavelich planned to establish an independent Croat state and that "a peaceful and partial solution" of that goal "was inadmissible."

Italy was up to her neck in instigating planned murders, and being assisted in this unworthy endeavor by Hungary. It was the authorities in Budapest who had extended an invitation for the Ustacha terrorists to operate from their country. And it was the Hungarians who provided them with passports and new identities so they could move freely all over the Continent on their assigned rounds of murder.

Hungary was no newcomer to the game of violence. She had been the host to the German Frei-Korps killers who had to leave their country in a hurry after they had killed Walter Rathenau and other prominent German democrats. She really entered a partnership with Italy when Julius Gomboes de Jafka became Prime Minister. Gomboes was an ethnic German whose name had been Knofe before he changed it. His parents had emigrated from the Rhineland. Like many members of minority groups they became violent and chauvinistic patriots. Gomboes was a super-Hungarian and an anti-Semite as well.

In his memoirs, the Regent, Nicholas Horty de Nabuyana, described Gomboes as an autocrat, remarking that "the example set by Hitler and Mussolini (had) made a profound impression on him."

Such an admirer of the two dictators could not help but be impressed by Ante Pavelich, the junior-league totalitarian. Admiration for his heroes did not long suffice. In time, Gomboes became an enthusiastic sponsor of the assassins.

In Berlin, Pavelich's newspaper contained a headline plain enough for anyone to understand: "Hide yourself, you gypsy! But it does not matter where you go. We will find you and kill you."

Alexander, a convinced pacifist, had become a fatalist about death. He once remarked that if he was to "die in my bed I shall have a less bloody end than most of my ancestors." He had witnessed the horrors of war first-hand, and he was determined to do all he could to prevent another conflict from breaking out in the Balkans.

During one of his more reflective moments he said, "There will be no war in the Balkans. The one danger has always been in the interference of the great powers in Balkan affairs. But for the meddling of the great powers there would not be even a shadow of the danger from this part of Europe."

When the King came to Zagreb late in the winter of 1933 he insisted that no unusual precautions should be taken to protect him. The police later discovered that Ustacha assassins had been within a few feet of him, but had not attacked because they lost their nerve at the last minute. That same evening the King walked with his friend Atsa Dimitrievich, among thousands of Croats crowding the streets. The police later told Alexander that he had been lucky to escape an assassin's bullet or bomb. Despite that warning, he took another walk on the streets of Zagreb. He also strolled on the main avenues of Sofia when he was on a state visit there.

Alexander was disturbed by the negative attitude the democracies had adopted toward the aggressive dictatorships. He was impressed by Barthou, who was determined to stand up to the Germans. In time, he hoped, Barthou would also conclude that Mussolini was not to be trusted.

Though Alexander was not a charter member of the Little

Entente, he approved of the alliance. The League of Nations could not keep the peace, but an alliance of states unafraid to fight to maintain it was the only hope the peoples of Europe had. Russia, that vast land peopled by Slavs, was now under the control of men with whose ideology he could not sympathize. Yet Russia had stood by Serbia when the Hapsburgs threatened to destroy the country. He knew that Czar Nicholas II, the "little father of all the Russias," had been instrumental in providing the ships that had transported the remnants of the defeated Serbian Army to Salonika. But the Russia of 1933–34 was not the Russia that had chased the Turks out of the Balkans and won freedom for the Slavs who inhabited the peninsula. The Bolshevik Government had never displayed any sympathy for Pan-Slavism. At least, though, it was committed to keeping the Nazis and the Fascists out of Eastern Europe.

The King had welcomed the White Russians into General Wrangel's Army after they had fled from their country in 1917–18. That gesture had no political connotation—Alexander was only trying to provide a haven for the refugees. Many of the Russians were engineers, and were given jobs in the nation's industries. Some were artists, and were put to work painting frescoes in churches. Others resumed teaching.

The rulers in the Kremlin were willing to overlook the political differences that existed between them and the leaders of the Little Entente. They realized that Alexander was motivated solely by a desire to maintain the peace. They were also convinced that he had given succour to the White Russians because he was a humanitarian at heart.

After Barthou had discussed an Eastern Locarno with Alexander, he instructed Yevtich to spell it out in detail for Benes and Titulescu. Benes told Yevtich that he was in favor of closer relations with the USSR. The politicians who were in power in Roumania, Yugoslavia, and Czechoslovakia now decided that they would cooperate closely on all matters pertaining to foreign policy. They agreed that there would be no separate pacts made without the consent of all the other nations comprising the Little Entente. The three nations would stand united against Italy and Hungary as well as Germany.

Mussolini and Hitler expressed their rage in no uncertain terms. Italy suddenly decided to play the role of a peace-loving power, and the Duce began to shout that the sexual degenerate in Berlin must be brought to heel. But Alexander suspected that his conversion to peace was only intended to delude the British and the French—Mussolini had not given up his plan to take over large areas of Yugoslavia.

The Duce had signed a non-aggression pact with the Russians on September 2, 1933. Alexander regarded it as mere Fascist window-dressing. Mussolini was still giving aid and comfort to the Ustacha and he was still encouraging Hungary to continue her anti-Yugoslav campaign. The King never forgot for one moment that the only way he could protect his Kingdom was to maintain strong relations with Bucharest, Prague, Paris and Moscow. Only if these Governments stood together could the aggressors be kept from overwhelming the Balkans.

12 *Alexander and Boris*

Alexander hoped to persuade his cousin King Boris of Bulgaria to break away from Italian influence and ally his country with Yugoslavia and the other member nations of the Little Entente. Boris was anxious to see his cousin Alexander and discover if it was possible to create a more harmonious atmosphere conducive to establishing better relations between their countries. Alexander agreed to see Boris, insisting, however, that he would meet him at the Belgrade railroad station.

Boris, having visited London, was on his way back to Sofia. He was told that the train he was on would stop in Belgrade, and that Alexander and his Queen and other dignitaries would be waiting there to receive him.

The Yugoslav people were happy to learn that their King was going to meet with the Bulgarian monarch. They too were anxious about the state of relations between their country and

Bulgaria. Boris' wife was the daughter of Queen Helena of Italy (a Montenegrin princess), making her the sister of Alexander's mother; she and the Yugoslav King had played together when they were children.

The Italian royal family had insisted that Boris' offspring should be raised as Roman Catholics. But his youngest child was baptized in the Orthodox faith. By that act Boris was telling the Italians that he did not favor Mussolini's adventurist policies. The men who were in power in the nations of the Little Entente now had reason to hope that Bulgaria would find her way into the anti-revisionist camp.

The royal meeting went off very well. Queen Joanna embraced her cousin and affectionately called him by his childhood nickname, Sandro. His icy demeanor melted and he relaxed. The royal couples sipped Turkish coffee and talked about family affairs. The bitter feeling that had separated them vanished; they were good friends again.

Alexander and Boris agreed that peace was essential so that both nations could prosper. The Bulgarians had previously projected the idea of a collective security pact to Yevtich when he was in Geneva. Alexander now broached the subject to Boris. But the Bulgarian King said that it was too early to come to any definite agreement: the I.M.R.O. was still a potent force in his country and its wings would have to be clipped before he could make any new commitments. Before he left Belgrade he assured his cousin that the terrorist society would be declared illegal at the proper time.

The two men reviewed one encouraging development: their countries had signed a commercial treaty on May 24, 1933, the first such between them since 1896. With an economic pact, there was good reason to hope that a political understanding would follow shortly.

A number of forward-looking politicians in both countries wanted to have Bulgaria become a part of Yugoslavia. Perhaps this would have come about if Yugoslavia had been a feder-

ated republic instead of a kingdom. The Bulgars could easily
have accepted a union if it were not to be dominated by a
Serbian royal house. Alexander thought the idea rather premature—it might become a political reality in one or two gen-
erations. As a realistic leader he could not indulge himself in
wishful fancies, but had to confine his political thinking to
current political realities.

The small nations of the Balkan peninsula had been victimized for decades by the major powers. Great Britain, France,
Austria and Russia and to some extent Germany had all had
their busy little hands in the Balkan pie. At this stage of history,
France and Russia wanted to maintain peace because they
were determined to maintain the status quo. It was therefore
safe for Alexander to enter into agreements with those powers.
But Italy, Hungary, and Germany were revisionist, and that
made it dangerous for Yugoslavia to give them any opportunity for betrayal.

Greece was afraid of the Fascist Italians threatening to invade her from their Albanian base. And Kemal Pasha, el
Ghazi, also had reasons to believe that the Fascists coveted
some of his territory.

Alexander, aware that Kemal Pasha was interested in coming to an arrangement with the Yugoslavs and the other members of the Little Entente, decided to go to the Turkish leader's
capital. He also wanted to talk again to the Roumanians. He
ordered his navy officers to ferry the *Dubrovnik* to Constanza
and await his arrival there. He got to Bucharest on September
30, and had a long discussion with King Carol. On October 3
he went to Constanza, boarded his destroyer, and sailed for
the Bulgarian port of Varna. King Boris and Queen Joanna
were at the Black Sea port to welcome him and Queen Marie,
and took them home to dinner at the palace. In a cordial discussion afterwards, Boris promised to try his best to convince
the Bulgar politicians that a friendly agreement between
Yugoslavia and his country would serve the interests of both
nations.

At eleven o'clock Alexander and Marie returned to the *Dubrovnik*. The destroyer entered the Bosporous the next morning: the city of Stamboul loomed straight ahead. When the royal couple stepped ashore they were greeted by thousands of Turks. A small boat drew alongside the *Dubrovnik* before the King left his destroyer. Ruzhdy Aras, a Turkish diplomat, climbed aboard and gave several huge bouquets of roses to the Queen.

It was to be a rather interesting day for Alexander. His Queen remained aboard the destroyer while her husband, dressed in his Admiral's uniform, was taken to Kemal's palace. Kemal, the military genius, wore a frock coat and his hands were covered by white gloves. He was apparently quite taken with his new friend.

Alexander, who lived like a Spartan in Belgrade, was overwhelmed by the luxurious splendor of el Ghazi's palace. The halls were all of alabaster. The sparkling crystal chandeliers blazed with an intensity that almost hurt the eyes. Priceless paintings covered the walls. Kemal's room was carpeted with expensive Oriental rugs. Alexander was served heavy Turkish coffee and sweets. He sipped the beverage while Kemal talked.

The hour got late, and Alexander indicated that he would like to return to his ship. Kemal accompanied him, and the two men found Queen Marie still awake. Her greeting quite charmed the Turkish leader. When she suggested that she wanted to tour the local wonders, Kemal said that the King and Queen had, as of then, the freedom of the city.

Next morning Marie and Alexander went to mosques, museums, and other landmarks. A tremendous crowd hailed them when they arrived at the Orthodox Cathedral of St. Sophia. After a brief rest back at the *Dubrovnik* late in the afternoon, they dressed for a special banquet arranged for them by Kemal at his palace.

The banquet was truly an event to be remembered. A bevy of extraordinarily beautiful women attended; none wore veils.

The orchestra played Turkish and Yugoslav music, and Le Jazz Hot. The food had been prepared by a famous French chef.

After the meal, Kemal and Alexander played some hands of poker. Queen Marie and Ismet Pasha, an intimate friend of el Ghazi, joined the game for a little while. Though Alexander won all the chips, he refused to take any money from the losers.

Kemal and the King adjourned to Kemal's chambers for a private conference, at which Alexander proposed that Turkey should join the Balkan alliance, a pact calling for all members to come to each other's assistance in case of attack by an aggressor. Kemal expressed eagerness to join; he also said that Turkey would fight alongside Yugoslavia if the Austrians or Italians attacked her. Kemal suggested that the Balkan Pact should be merged with the Little Entente Pact, and extended to include the USSR in an overall agreement.

Alexander left Turkey the following morning, pleased that the atmosphere had been so cordial. Next stop was Corfu, where the King visited the cemetery of the Greek and Yugoslav soldiers who had laid down their lives during the Salonika campaign. Then he returned to the city to await news from the Yugoslav Ambassador in Athens, who had been delegated to discuss a treaty with the Greeks. The report was that Greek Premier Maximos had said he was ready to join any pact that would assure the safety of his country.

On this trip, Alexander also made some secret contacts with the Albanians. The mountain people were becoming increasingly restive under the Italian military occupation of their country. He assured Tirana that Yugoslavia had no ambitions to take over the smaller nation. He also told the Albanians that he would give his support when they moved to dislodge the Italian troops and chase them home.

The Balkan Pact was signed by the Premier of Greece in Athens on November 27, 1933. At the same moment, Alexander was also signing a copy of the same document in Belgrade, and the Turkish Foreign Minister was affixing his signature to the agreement in Istanbul. The Bulgarians promised to join the others in the near future.

The signing of the Pact was greeted with derision by Mussolini and his Hungarian friends. The Duce was now determined to get rid of the King, and Barthou as well. These men were blocking him from expanding his Fascist empire into the Balkans.

In Berlin, Eugene Kvaternik was seeing Alfred Rosenberg, Hitler's advisor on foreign affairs. He was also in contact with Heinrich Himmler. The Nazis, too—frustrated by Alexander and his French friends—were encouraging the Ustacha to continue its subversive activities. They permitted Kvaternik to publish a newspaper in Berlin. The *Nezavisla Hrvatska Drzava (Independent Croatian State)* was urging its readers to kill all foreign statesmen who stood in the way of Pavelich. It printed the text of a resolution calling for the murder of the King. One edition of the paper headlined a report that "the bomb that will kill the King of Yugoslavia is now being manufactured." In its issue of August 16, 1934, a few months before the double killing in Marseilles, *Hrvatska Drzava* published an article giving details of the agreement the Little Entente had concluded with France. It accused Louis Barthou of being an enemy of the Croatian people, and it also accused King Alexander, Benes, and Titulescu of pursuing a policy of enslaving nations. The story concluded with a threat: "Soon the day will come when the people of Croatia at the call of their leader will take up arms to wash off this shame with blood."

Barthou, who had once said that a public servant has to expect attack, took little note of that threat. Alexander, who wasn't afraid of death, took no notice of it. The Fascists and the Ustacha could not frighten either man. But they had marked them for death nevertheless.

13 Barthou Mends More Diplomatic Fences

[decorative border]

Barthou and Maxim Litvinoff, the rotund little Soviet Foreign Minister, had a clear understanding about the best means of containing an aggressive Germany. Litvinoff told Barthou that security could best be achieved by organizing the nations that stood for peace into various pacts. He agreed that France, the USSR, the Little Entente and the Baltic States should become signatories of an Eastern Locarno Pact. And then, working in concentric circles, he wanted to include the Greeks, the Turks, and possibly the Italians in a Mediterranean Pact. The major naval powers would then be included in still another pact. In that way all the nations including the United States would have become members of a league dedicated to preserving the peace.

Barthou had now succeeded in bringing the Little Entente and Russia together. All were in accord about the necessity of an Eastern Locarno. Alexander had proved himself a worthy political ally of Barthou. Both knew that Hitler represented a danger to their countries. But there were many Frenchmen so blinded by hatred of the Russians that they were ready for a sellout rather than have the Kremlin as an ally. And if that entailed the destruction of France's alliances with the nations of Eastern Europe, they were ready to face up to that as well.

Barthou was no political neophyte. He knew what he was doing. He had served his country for more than four decades— ever since the time when he was first elected a national deputy in 1889—and his understanding of foreign relations was profound. He had been Minister of the Interior in the Meline Cabinet, and at the age of thirty-two he had been appointed Minister of Public Works and Garde des Sceau, serving successively in the cabinets of Sarrien, Clemenceau, and Briand.

On March 29, 1913, Raymond Poincaré asked him to form a government. During 1917 he was a Minister in the Painleve Administration. After the First World War he was Clemenceau's close associate and worked with the Tiger and Poincaré to preserve the victory. He also acted as Rapporteur of the Chamber of Deputies Commission to report on the Versailles Treaty. He was Minister of Justice in the Poincaré Government of National Union, and in a number of Briand administrations. But it was not until 1934, after a long period of inactivity, that he was asked to accept the post of Foreign Minister in the Doumergue Government.

Barthou could read and write German like a native, and he was thoroughly conversant with German literature and music. He was one of the few statesmen who had read *Mein Kampf* in the original language. He never thought of it as a mere propaganda tract; he said that the fanatic had told the world just what he had in store for it. And because he was so keenly aware of Hitler's long-range plans for France, Barthou would never barter away his country's security even when he was pressured by the British to be more flexible in his attitude toward Berlin.

French Governments had, in the past, made many concessions to the Germans. Too many, according to Barthou. Now, the Germans were in the ascendant again, and if Hitler succeeded in his purpose, proud France would be reduced to the position of a third-rate power.

Barthou was simply following France's traditional policies when he urged his country to align herself with the Russians. Edouard Herriot had signed a non-aggression pact with the Muscovites back in 1931. The French people had approved of it and welcomed Litvinoff with enthusiasm when he came to Paris in July 1933.

Pierre Cot, the Air Minister, had gone to Moscow that same year and been well treated by his Russian hosts. The Kremlin, strangely enough, had just signed an agreement with the Germans. When Baron Rothschild asked why the Russians were flirting with the Germans, they explained their behavior quite logically.

"Well, you see, it's like this. France and Great Britain are two eminently respectable old ladies who would not think of harming us. But there is one country in Europe which has the power to do us harm, only one country which we fear, and that is Germany. Now we hate Germany so much that we are perfectly capable of forming an alliance with her merely in order to rouse France and Great Britain from their lethargy, which makes them inclined to get along with her [Germany] and start them fighting our enemy for us."

While Barthou was creating a diplomatic cordon around the Third Reich and attempting to flatter the Duce, the terrorists had been busily engaged in finding a way of getting rid of him. The life of a democratic leader was always in danger of being snuffed out in the early 1930s. When Barthou was a passenger on the Strasbourg-Paris Rapide on his way back to France from his Eastern European tour, the train stopped for a few minutes at the Nancy railroad station. M. Cornier, the Inspector of Special Police, who was acting as Barthou's body-guard, wired ahead to Paris that at 8:20 A.M. someone had thrown a large rock into the car. A stone aimed better could have seriously injured the Foreign Minister. Another time, when a train he was traveling on passed through Austria, some local Nazis tried to bomb it.

Barthou had no time to think about the dangers he faced. But he did devote a great deal of time to worrying about the British and their attitude toward Germany. Stanley Baldwin and Sir John Simon were apparently disposed to grant the Reich more armaments. Germany had been secretly rearming for years. The Western democratic politicians were well aware of what was going on in the Reich, but preferred to look the other way—and nothing was happening there. The British stance finally provoked Lord Ponsonby to declare that his country was engaged in a long series of vacillating evasions. Neither Baldwin nor any other British leader, he said, was making "any serious attempt at calling the world to reason after the great tragedy it had been through."

His Government, Ponsonby alleged, was "supplying Germany with arms in private while protesting that Germany was rearming." And then he expressed a wish that "some Polar expedition being prepared, that would be away for two or three years," would include Simon and the PM.

"The sigh of relief that would go up in this country would be audible far and wide," he exclaimed to the cheers of the more militant Labour Members.

Anthony Eden had been sent to Berlin to discuss current problems with Hitler. The meeting was an interesting one. The Reich was represented by Hitler himself, Baron von Neurath (the German Foreign Minister), and General Blomberg (the Minister of Defense and Chief of the General Staff).

Eden and Hitler talked about their common experiences in the trenches during World War I. They studied a map of

France and discovered to their obvious delight that they had been facing each other on the front during most of the conflict.

Eventually, Hitler brought up the rearmament problem. Eden thought he was taking a reasonable attitude. The Führer wanted an army of 300,000 men, and a fair number of scouting and pursuit planes. The new army would have to be equipped with modern weapons. He assured Eden that the Storm Troopers would not be armed.

In a letter to Eduard Benes (later found in Cezch archives captured by the Germans after they had invaded the country), Thomas Masaryk told his close associate that he had had lunch with Eden, who had been as cautious in his private remarks as in the parliament speech in which he reported his conversations with the Führer.

"It is worth noting," wrote Masaryk, "that Eden had a five-hour talk with Hitler and that Hitler . . . made a good impression on him. Eden considers him to be a sincere fanatic who does not want war. My personal impression is that the recent promotion to Lord Privy Seal and the trip to Europe have gone to Eden's head a little. He is comparatively young and life has spoilt him."

The Parisian newspapers criticized Eden severely. But the German Government and press gave him unstinted praise. The *Völkischer Beobachter* and the *Boersen Zeitung* suggested that Paris had overlooked the conciliatory spirit and the peaceful will of the German people—who would, if no clear reply came from Paris on rearmament, have to do what honor demanded and act "in accordance with the primitive needs of German national security and that which has been acknowledged as facts by the British and Italian governments."

Trouble appeared to loom for Barthou not only in England but in Belgium as well. During January 1934, Senator (Baron) René de Dordolot, a Conservative deputy from Charleroi, convinced his Party leaders that a declaration should be issued calling for control of German rearmament. He gave Barthou the "order du jour" on February 16. Barthou asked Dordolot whether Belgium would contribute any armed units if France decided to march her army into Germany. Dordolot assured Barthou that Belgium would cooperate with France. The deputy also said that Belgian Conservatives would demand the retirement of the appeasement-minded Foreign Minister Paul Hymans. There would be a new ministry, and it would support the French position.

Barthou informed Dordolot that France planned to expose the facts of Germany's secret rearming. He was certain that once the information was made public, Europe would be shocked. The French Government was telling the Reich that all her secretly manufactured armaments should be destroyed. When Dordolot asked what France intended to do if Hitler defied her, Barthou replied that the army would be ordered to march into the Rhineland.

Dordolot, pleased by that answer, told Barthou that the Belgian Senate would probably go along with the French and order Belgium's troops to invade the Reich. But fate was to intervene to frustrate the desire for forceful action by the Belgian deputy and the French Foreign Minister. King Albert, who had been put on the Reich's list as a public enemy, was killed while on vacation. Albert had been expected to approve of Barthou's plan; he had never trusted the Germans, and his wife, Queen Elisabeth, a member of the Bavarian royal house of Wittelsbach, had had enough experiences with her former countrymen during the war to distrust them even more than her husband did.

With the untimely demise of King Albert, the appeasement-oriented Belgian Government began to sabotage the Barthou-Dordolot policy. The nation went into a period of mourning for their deceased ruler. The parliament was closed, and not reconvened until March 6. Premier Charles de Broqueville told Dordolot that he wanted to deliver the first speech. Since the Premier was the head of the Government, Dordolot had to agree to let him make it.

Broqueville castigated the men who were advocating an

invasion of the Reich. "The remedy," he said, "is worse than the evil, and it could only be envisaged by someone touched by folly or with a criminal mentality. I refuse," he shouted, "to launch this country into such an adventure. The more obvious solution is a modus vivendi with Germany, to be arrived at through negotiations for a minimum of sacrifice in return for a maximum of guarantees. The present situation is the consequence of a great illusion to keep a great nation in a disarmed state indefinitely."

That speech pre-dated the Chamberlain kowtowing to Hitler. Germany was armed to the teeth: Generals Groener and von Seeckt had directed the operation right under the collective noses of the Inter-Allied Control Commission. The Versailles Treaty had been violated before its ink had dried. German officers had been training men in Russia, and airplane factories had been established there during the early 1920s. Krupp was manufacturing heavy guns and other armaments, and the visionary Broqueville was telling his people that a nation like Germany had a right to rearm. They had already rearmed. The absence of King Albert was sorely felt by the people that day. The Premier would never have dared to advocate a pro-German policy had Albert been alive.

Events in Brussels pleased Adolf Hitler very much. His newspapers heaped mountains of praise on Broqueville and extolled him to the skies. The *Berliner Tageblatt* saw "the end of an illusion." The *Neue Preussische Kreuz Zeitung* announced that Versailles was "over."

The Catholic and Flemish newspapers in Belgium eulogized the Premier and advocated that Germany should be made a friend of the country. But the liberal *Le Soir, Nation,* and *Belge Peuple* disagreed with the Premier's premise.

The *Belge Peuple* said of the Premier's statements: "It is certain that this country will not be without profound emotion and condemn this admission by the chief of the government that we ought to appease Germany and to abandon all hope of obliging Germany to respect the formal clauses of the treaty which was paid for with 30,000 of our dead."

The editors wanted to know whether "British blindness to German rearmament was not better proof of the *mentalité criminale* in Europe."

Paul Hymans, the Foreign Minister, told David Morris, the American Ambassador, "The speech should not be interpreted as showing any alteration in the foreign policy pursued by Belgium during the past three months."

Hymans, who should have known better, was also advocating that Germany be permitted to rearm.

Poland had been the first nation to swallow Hitler's bait, and had encouraged him to become more demanding. And now Belgium was doing the same.

This was not the worst of that fateful year. To those who listened to the Members of Parliament in London on March 14, it was clear that there were many appeasers in high places.

Eden declared that his Government could not take a definite position on the disarmament question before it could ascertain what the French had in mind. That was equivocating with a vengeance since he knew exactly what Barthou was thinking and what conclusions he had drawn on the question.

Eden said that he had discussed the problem with many of Europe's leaders during his recent tour of the Continent.

"Is it the experience of my mission that it is hopeless to try and reconcile them?" He was talking about the differences on disarmament between Germany and France. And without waiting for a response from the House he said, "The answer is no definitely. Until we are in possession of all the replies to our memorandum it is premature to be so pessimistic . . . but it is definitely wrong to paint the picture darker than it is. While there is a glimmer of light we will not admit defeat, and there is more than a glimmer."

The Conservatives and the Labourites must have been puzzled by his remarks that day. Was he talking about political problems on the Continent, or was he giving them a lecture in astronomy?

He admitted, "The mission was an impossible task which would commend to France an elaborate scheme of disarmament which meant that the French should be no stronger than Poland, Germany or Italy. It would be an error in diplomatic policy to press a matter when it is clear that no further progress is made."

Why then, the question was heard in the land, had he not stayed home instead of junketing all over Europe discussing weighty political problems with Hitler, Barthou, and Mussolini?

Winston Churchill, who never had any illusions about Hitler, said that Eden's statements on competitive armament offered no real security for Britain or for Europe. "False ideas have been spread in this country that disarmament means peace," he said. "The disarmament conference has brought us steadily nearer to a pronounced state of ill-will than anything else that could be imagined. I pointed out four years ago that the pressing of disarmament on nations who had already disarmed and who had signified in one way or another their desire not to be pressed further was most dangerous diplomacy.

"After futile conferences what have you got? The rearmament of Germany—that is the monstrous child which has emanated from this immense labor. There is something to be said for isolation. There is something to be said for alliances. But there is nothing to be said for weakening the powers on the Continent with whom you would be in alliance, and then involving yourself more in Continental tangles in order to make it up to them. The Romans had a maxim—'shorten your weapons and lengthen your frontiers.' But ours seems to be: diminish your weapons and increase your obligations, aye, and diminish the weapons of your friends."

The realism of Churchill was not matched by Thomas

Masaryk, who, in a letter to a friend, wrote: "The Churchill address did not make any impression in Parliament. It is known everywhere that Winston is going through a stage of alarming psychology and is continually calling attention to the possibility of war and the necessity of armaments."

Two top Nazis were blunt in their reactions. Captain Ernst Röhm, notorious homosexual organizer of the Storm Troopers, warned the French, "Any illegal attack on the Reich [will] entail so great a risk that any aggressor would have to seriously consider whether the possible gains would be worth the risks." And Hermann Goering said that there would be "no easy walk into the Rhineland."

Both these men were whistling in the dark. They knew the German Army was too weak to offer any serious resistance if the French marched into the Rhineland. That fact was confirmed when Hitler's generals testified before the Nuremberg Trials. One Junker commander said that the army had been ordered to retreat from the territory when the French moved in. The army, according to this testimony, would have been defeated in a few days.

Despite the certain knowledge that Britain and France still held all the aces in the deck, London appeared to have adopted a timid attitude toward Hitler. The Cliveden Set was advocating a Be Kind to the Germans policy. Important newspapers compared Barthou to Raymond Poincaré, and accused both men of persecuting the Germans. Many Labourites felt that Germany should be allowed to rearm, while others accused Barthou of seeking to destroy the Reich.

Barthou tried to explain that his Eastern Locarno Pact was not an alliance but a mutual-security agreement. He emphasized that Germany had been invited to join with France and the nations of Eastern Europe in an anti-aggression agreement. He assured the British that he did not want one of her soldiers to participate in a war, but desired only England's moral support. His aims were clear enough, but the politicians at Whitehall were more suspicious of the real purposes of France than they were of the Germans.

Hitler was quite certain that the British Government would not cooperate with Barthou. In the end, he was proven to be correct. Joachim von Ribbentrop, the Führer's traveling salesman, who served as his Commissioner on Disarmament Questions, told him that many of the most important British politicians had expressed their sympathy for the German position. Hitler had proposed that all the nations of Europe including Britain should "renounce the use of force," and promised that Germany would sign a non-aggression pact. The British believed him, accusing Barthou of being a vindictive Frenchman simply following the policy of his old mentor, Georges Clemenceau. They refused to see that Barthou, having to be concerned with the security of his country, was willing to grant Germany more arms if she agreed to submit to a probationary period during which an International Commission would check her armaments plants for violations. Hitler refused to concede on that point. He threatened to produce weapons which had been forbidden Germany: big guns, tanks, and combat planes.

At the Disarmament Conference, André Tardieu proposed a comprehensive plan for a reduction of one-third in arms and the complete destruction of tanks, mobile guns, and planes. The British did not present any concrete ideas, but Sir John Simon, speaking in the name of his Government, offered a minor stipulation. He suggested the appointment of a committee empowered to decide what weapons "were offensive and what were not." That was one way of sidetracking the issue. Germany withdrew from the Conference, and one year later she left the League of Nations.

Why did the British persist in believing that Hitler was a man of peace? The Nazi bible, in its original language, had been explicit enough about his real aims. On page 699 of *Mein Kampf* the Führer stated that he would propose an alliance with England and Italy and then have both countries agree to allow him a free hand in Eastern Europe. He told his readers that England could never tolerate having Germany become a world power, and that war between the Reich and the island empire was inevitable. The first task of the Reich Government was to have patience, to expand the nation and take over Austria, the Sudetenland, and all other areas populated by Germans. After the new acquisitions had been thoroughly digested, Germany would smash Russia, and then turn west again and attack Britain.

The British were unrealistic about Italy, also. They could have learned better if they had listened to what Dino Grandi, Italian Minister of Foreign Affairs, had to say about his country's future plans. At the 1932 Disarmament Conference he said, "We claim the right of expansion of Italy and the abolishing of the present order in Europe. Otherwise forty million Italians—which will be fifty million in fifteen years—will be crowded to death on an inland sea."

The Reich's compulsive urge to expand into other people's territory pre-dated Hitler by many years. Franz von Papen, Chancellor of the Reich before General Schleicher managed to pull the rug out from under him, had enlightened the Reichstag about the real needs of the nation. He said, "It is our desire to abolish the parliamentary regime in Germany, subdue the forces in our country which are hostile to us, and in international politics we demand the freedom to expand, and the rearmament of the Reich."

After repeated failure to come to any understanding at the various disarmament conferences, Ribbentrop suddenly made an appearance in Paris, shortly after Hitler had met with Mussolini. The Commissioner demanded an appointment with Doumergue and Barthou. He saw Barthou; it was the first time a French statesman had consented to discuss the disarmament problem with a German politician person-to-person. Despite the best efforts of the ex-wine salesman, Barthou was not convinced that Germany should be permitted to rearm without a probationary period of supervision by an outside body of experts. "The door is still open on the disarmament issue," he told Ribbentrop. "Take your proposals to Geneva, where they will be examined with the impartiality they merit because of their determining influence on the peace of Europe."

Barthou was far too clever to be ensnared into a Nazi trap. In a fit of desperation Ribbentrop urged von Koestler to arrange a meeting with Doumergue. That old politician was able to resist the rather heavy-handed flattery of the Commissioner, and refused to discuss any of the pending problems. He reminded Ribbentrop that all diplomatic matters were handled by Barthou, his Foreign Minister. Even Ribbentrop, not a very astute man, realized that he was being made a victim of buck-passing—French style.

The French knew how to cope with the Nazi menace. But the British were still trying to direct a balancing act in between France and Germany. When Ribbentrop went to London toward the middle of November of 1933, he tried to convince Sir John Simon that "the rearmament of Germany had no aggressive purposes and was only to provide the country with defensive arms up to her requirements."

Paris had decided that since the Reich had rearmed to a large extent already, it would be sensible to recognize that fact and have France accept it. But Barthou did not intend to give Germany a legal basis for her actions.

Although Barthou had to contend with many enemies among his own countrymen, there were a few who agreed with his policies. One such friend was Louis de Chappedelaine. During a debate in the Chamber of Deputies Chappedelaine said that the Nazi regime was undoubtedly passing through a serious crisis requiring certain "distracting moves abroad." He told his colleagues that there were 20,000 German soldiers at the Austrian frontier, and that the Reich had an army of 400,000 men which could easily be increased to a million in 48 hours.

The Nazis were building fortifications in the demilitarized zones across the Rhine, and 300,000 soldiers were inside the territory. He pointed out that Krupp had increased its production of armaments since the withdrawal of the Inter-Allied Control Mission.

The French Socialists, who might have known better, adopted a very unrealistic position on the disarmament question. Chassergue, a Socialist deputy, charged that the Government had broken with the "traditional approach of France to the question of disarmament and left France isolated, costing her the support of Britain and the United States and throwing her back to her old alliances with Czechoslovakia and Poland."

Chassergue also accused Barthou of having taken an unreasonable attitude on the whole problem. The French Foreign Minister, he said, stood for an arms race and "no more negotiations" with the Germans.

Barthou was continually badgered by both the Right and the Left. The Left accused him of being a warmonger, while the Right said that he was pro-Russian. He for his part merely kept repeating that "France must place in the forefront of her preoccupation the conditions of her own security, which, moreover, she does not separate from that of other interested powers. This attitude must continue even before France seeks to discover whether an agreement can be obtained upon a system of guarantees of execution which would legalize a substantial rearmament of Germany."

Hitler now lost his patience with the French and with the League of Nations. He ordered his diplomats to walk out of the League. He told his people that Germany would be kept in a subservient position as long as she remained in an organization that was dominated by the "Versailles criminals." He did not tell the Germans that the League would have gone along with a supervised rearmament and that he had refused to be checked upon by any Commission.

Barthou took the position that the Reich's return to the

League would make possible an equitable system of "guar-antees of execution." That suggestion was greeted by complete silence on the part of the German leaders; Barthou observed that "in this respect the course of recent communications does not permit of better hopes." He insisted that German return to the League was "an essential condition of the signature of a disarmament convention."

France, he declared, "would not abandon this essential and necessary condition . . . at the very moment when German rearmament is being claimed, prepared and developed without any account being taken of negotiations entered upon in ac-cordance with the wishes of Germany itself."

The Socialist leader Léon Blum, later to distinguish himself in the Spanish Civil War by clamping down a blockade which worked against the embattled Spanish Republicans, now came to the fore with a declaration in which he accused Barthou of having "isolated France in international opinion." Blum, as usual, had evaluated the international situation incorrectly. There were others who expressed their confidence in Barthou's foreign policy.

The prestigious *Le Temps*, reputed to be a Government mouthpiece, said that Barthou's remarks had "frankness, logic and firmness of tone." Vladimir d'Ormesson, the political pun-dit, assured his countrymen that "we can have complete confi-dence in the clairvoyance of our Foreign Minister."

Barthou responded to the Blum statements by saying that no country could consider itself to be isolated if it had such fast friends as Czechoslovakia, Roumania, Yugoslavia, Greece, and Turkey.

Peace, he said, "could only be assured if all nations respected treaties and also stood by the League of Nations." He declared that if France granted the Reich the right to rearm without supervision it would be courting defeat in a war.

André Simon, in a book published a number of years after the Marseilles murders, recalled that Barthou had said, "If we take the fatal step we shall be faced with new and higher demands in a short time. One day, we shall have to make a stand. It is better that we make it now while the trump cards are still in our hands."

The strength of France, he said, rested on her army and on her allies in the Balkans, Russia, and Britain. He still had confidence that London could be made to see that a Nazi Reich could never be appeased.

Barthou hoped that Hitler's actions would open the eyes of the British leaders and make them understand what the Führer had in mind for Europe. He could see that Hitler would never sign an Eastern Locarno treaty; presumably, his refusal to do so would expose the Reich as a state bent on aggression.

Barthou believed that the Russian Army was powerful enough to stand up against the Germans. France, alone, could easily have crushed Hitler's army back in 1933–34. Russia later demonstrated that her army could stop the Teutonic hordes.

Some French politicians—Barthou had to listen to them— still believed that there was a good and a bad Germany. The good Germany was represented by men like Gustav Stresemann, the old monarchist-nationalist, who had managed to convince Aristide Briand that he was a peace-loving statesman. The bad, according to those Frenchmen who saw that distinction in the Reich, was represented by a Hitler, a von Papen, a Hugenberg. The good Germany would prevail in the end— or so they hoped. Barthou never distinguished two Germanys; as far as he was concerned there was only one Reich and its true face was aggressive nationalism.

The Right in France tried to convince him that a Hitler-ruled Reich was more to be trusted than a Russia. They reacted predictably when he invited the Soviets to become part of the League of Nations.

Charles Maurras, the former anarchist turned royalist and anti-Semite, said that the Quai d'Orsay needed to be trained again "to be distrustful of the various songs of the Moscow

siren." Barthou, according to him, was "not capable of recall-
ing the Quai d'Orsay to its good senses." Maurras was later to
become pro-Fascist and pro-Nazi and a pillar of the Vichy
Regime during the German occupation.

Pierre Cot, who could have pondered the problem better
before he spoke, said that Barthou was an advocate of old and
hoary policies. "If the policy of pacts is not accompanied by
a general controlled reduction of armaments—if it should proceed without German participation, then it would be necessary
to call this policy by its true name, a policy of alliances, and
we reject this policy at any price. We have not waged war to
return to the old politique of alliances and armaments. This I
say quite plainly to those men who merely assisted at the
spectacle of our massacred youth."

What a blow below the belt! How could Barthou direct a
policy of "general controlled reduction of armaments" if Hitler
categorically refused to discuss it? And why was it necessary
to accuse Barthou of not being a soldier in the war? His son
Max—his only son—eighteen years old, was killed while serving his country.

Cot, an aviator and a knowledgeable and well-intentioned
man, knew that Germany had been violating the Versailles
Treaty for years. He should have noted one sentence in *Mein
Kampf:* "An alliance whose aim does not include the intention
of war is worthless nonsense."

Reich Commissioner Hermann Goering also had some revealing things to say about German ambitions, in a speech made
in Essen: "For the living it is a holy duty to fulfill the mission for which Germans have given their lives in the war. If no
other way can be found, they must be ready to redeem with
blood a pledge written in blood."

Franz von Papen, ex-saboteur and a member of the Herren-
klub, had his own pertinent remarks about war: "A philosopher
had said that he was no man who was not a father; it was even
more true that she was not a woman who was not a mother.

The maintenance of eternal life demands the sacrifice of the individual. Mothers must exhaust themselves in order to give life to children. Fathers must fight on the battlefield in order to secure the future of their sons."

A declaration by the Women's Order of the Red Swastika included a rousing message: "There is no higher or finer privilege for a woman than that of sending her children to war."

And if that wasn't enough, there was the frank statement in *Wirtschaftsdienst*, an important German economic journal, that France's efforts to prevent bloodletting depended in large measure on what Hitler would do. Germany was opposed to an Eastern Locarno, the paper said, because it would bolster the status quo in Eastern Europe and become still another obstacle to the "freedom of action of Germany and Poland eastward."

A country with spokesmen like these could never be led into more peaceful pursuits. Barthou did not have to be told that Germany was on the road to war unless she was stopped from her mad ambitions by France and her allies. He had expected that Hitler would turn down his invitation to join an Eastern Locarno. Once the Führer had clearly indicated that he intended to go his own way, Barthou would be able to fall back on a purely military arrangement with the Little Entente, Russia, Greece, and the Turks. The British would be forced to go along in the end, and Belgium would learn in time that France's cause was her own as well.

Poland, too, would recover her wits and repudiate her ten-year non-aggression pact with the Nazi Regime. Barthou knew, however, that it would not happen as long as Colonel Beck was serving as Foreign Minister. He still recalled Beck's display of bad manners when Maxim Litvinoff stood under the floodlights delivering his acceptance of and expressing his gratitude for France's invitation to Russia to become a member of the League of Nations. Beck, standing in the shadows, sneered, "All this is nothing. It's the Third International being welcomed by the Second." The President of the League's Assembly at the time was the Swedish Socialist Sandler.

Barthou had a very stormy session with Beck that day. Poland, the Colonel said, refused to guarantee the territorial integrity of Czechoslovakia and Lithuania. In effect, he was telling the French that his country would play the role of the jackal when the Germans invaded either nation.

Bilmanis, the Latvian Ambassador to Moscow, and Lozaraitis, the Foreign Minister of Lithuania, told Barthou that their governments would join France in an Eastern Locarno regardless of any actions the Poles or the Germans might take against them.

By that time, Hitler and Mussolini had reached a conclusion about Louis Barthou. The two dictators could see he was a clear and present danger to them both.

On April 17, 1934, Barthou wrote a note to London in which he tried to clarify his policy once again. He told the British Government leaders that his purpose was to achieve security for France. But London remained unconvinced about France's intentions; there was still fear of having France dominate the Continent. The men in charge thought a lasting peace could be attained only if all the nations of Europe agreed to reduce their armaments to the lowest point compatible with the preservation of the European balance of power. And the same politicians thought that the balance could best be preserved by permitting the Germans to rearm, offsetting the power that was wielded by France.

14 *Barthou and the British*

Ante Pavelich had been at war with Alexander and his Serbs for a long time. He knew that as long as Europe remained at peace there was very little likelihood of his being able to tear Croatia away from Yugoslavia. But the Italian Fascist Government was clearly girding its loins for war. Mussolini announced his new budget. New armaments had an allocation of $84,150,000—a substantial increase over the preceding year's expenditures for military hardware. Hitler's establishment had already made public its own military budget, including a very large sum for arms.

The Belgians, toying with their new concept of neutrality, became alarmed. Paul Hymans, their dapper little Foreign Minister, approached the French and asked if they would fight if his country was invaded. The French Government told him that it would honor its commitments as a signatory of the

Locarno Pact. Paris really had no choice. The German Army moving across Belgium would probably ram its way through the extremely vulnerable Ardennes-Mons sector and outflank the Maginot Line.

The nervous diplomat who, a short time before, had been so enthusiastic an apostle of the appeasement of Germany, had a long discussion with Sir George Clerk, the British Ambassador in Brussels. Asked if Britain would fight in the event of a German attack, the Ambassador assured Hymans that she would. Hymans, however, still had his doubts about England. He contacted Long and was told there was nothing to fear. Yet a few days later, Sir John Simon told Hymans that he was "not prepared to favor sanctions against Germany if Britain was requested to do so." He advised Hymans not to inform Paris about their conversations or about the tentative agreements between Belgium and Britain. London was ready to protect Belgium, but it had no intention of making any commitments to Paris. Van Zuylen, an important Low Country diplomat, said that Britain "nourished strong fears against France." Apparently she did: Simon had said his country did not wish "France to ask the same thing of us."

During the late spring of 1934, in Geneva, Hymans had a lengthy conversation with Simon, who advised Belgium to conclude a non-aggression pact with the Germans. Hymans was surprised, and wanted to know whether such an accord would weaken the Locarno Pact. Simon declared that it would remind the Reich of its own obligations incurred at Locarno. A Belgian-German non-aggression pact would facilitate an Anglo-Belgian accord in the near future.

Shortly after trying to convince Hymans to keep France in the dark about London's Belgian policies, Simon delivered a speech in Geneva. He insisted on speaking ahead of Barthou, to the great annoyance of the Frenchman. "An international agreement about armaments would be meaningless without

German participation," he said. The only solution he saw was to have France support a modification of the disarmament pact.

And in an appeasement vein: "The only thing that matters now is an agreement." The conference must choose, he said, between "either limited but real reduction in arms made side by side with moderate rearmament or pure and simple limitation of the status quo accompanied by rearmament on a large scale." Germany, he said, "insisted upon rearming and we will not lend ourselves to indefinite continuance of vague and inconclusive discussions."

The seemingly reasonable attitude that Simon had adopted was only a means of covering up a policy of knuckling under to the German demand for more arms.

Barthou responded to the Simon speech with one of his own, tinged with sarcasm. His face was flushed with anger and his usually mellow voice had a sharp edge to it.

"It is not only the authority of the disarmament conference that is at stake; to speak plainly it is the conference's very existence. Perhaps I should add that over and above the disarmament conference which is the emanation of the Council of the League of Nations, the very existence of the League may prove at stake during the session."

He reminded Simon, and the American representative, Norman Davis, that "Security (was) the basis of the disarmament question." He quoted a number of remarks that had been made previously by both men in which they had expressed their fear of the Reich.

"Is the situation different now?" he asked. "Difficulties must not be hidden under vague optimistic phrases. What happened next? Germany left the conference. Does that mean that the principles of October 14 . . . are no longer valid?

"After prolonged efforts certain powers had agreed upon a reasonable and accepted system. Germany refused to accept it.

Is it because of Germany that the system be declared inaccept-
able? Have matters come to such a pass that there is a power
which is both invisible and present—present, if I may use the
metaphor, by the very absence—which is not participating in
the conference, which had left the League, which in consequence will be faced with no responsibility and which will
have all the rights without any of the corresponding duties?

"Is the embargo—the word is fashionable at present—of that
power to prevent the League and the disarmament conference
from reaching a conclusion? Have we come to the point where
there is only one system to be discussed? I am well aware that
paternity has its illusions. My honored colleague, Sir John
Simon, has devised a plan and this has been set forth in the
United Kingdom memorandum of January 29 (1934). The
illusion of his paternity is so great that he has gone so far as
to say that only one concrete plan has been submitted to the
General Disarmament Commission.

"How can it be said that there is only one plan? I fully
realize the importance of the United Kingdom plan, but Mussolini who is certainly capable of paternity has also a child.
The child is strong and well made, as Sir John Simon should
well know since it has been . . . in his hands (since) January 4.
But is it not possible for Sir John to be not only a good father
but a good godfather as well? In any case the plan exists and
has received the attention of the French Government's Foreign
Minister. I speak collectively because it is not long since action
to establish paternity has been permitted in France.

"France (also) has had a child and that child was born on
January 1, 1934, and Boncour has been its godfather. How
could it be asserted that there is nothing concrete in the
French plan of January first? For my part I think that other
plans than the United Kingdom plan exist. France stopped
negotiations when the German budget was published. France
reduced by seventeen per cent its military credits during
1932–34. Germany increased its military budget thirty-three

per cent and 160 per cent in aviation. Why? Who threatened Germany? I am speaking of a country for whose greatness I cannot conceal my sincere admiration—a country that has produced some of the geniuses in the history of mankind: Kant, Goethe, Bach, Beethoven and Wagner. Why deny that country not merely its intellectual power but that equality which is necessary in social life and in economic life, and which it has every right to claim? Who is threatening Germany? Certainly not France.

"Our plan for a limitation of armaments, dated January 1, 1934, is in your files. Why refuse to discuss it and so condemn it by a formula that abolishes it? Do we mean that there is nothing to be done, that we have produced the final truth, some sort of expression of some sort of infallible dogma?

"I am not a visionary nor am I disillusioned. I do not believe in miracles, but I do not cry out that all is lost. Reference is made, in meetings such as the present one, to prophets. There are two kinds of prophets to which the League of Nations must refuse to listen. There are in the first place confirmed optimists who deny the cruel evidence of the most urgent peril; and there are the pessimists who refuse to admit that there is any hope. Between the two there is room for men of action, who, having declared war on war, wish to save in peace and through peace, what is the greatest and not the least in humanity."

Barthou's eloquence was wasted on the British Government. One London newspaper took him to task for having alluded to the subject of paternity during a serious discussion. It accused him of having given a display of very poor taste at the least.

Barthou had asked for a trial period of four years to test the Germans before any nations should be asked to destroy their stockpile of arms. He reminded the British that there were Nazi garrisons in the Rhineland, and that the S.S. and S.A. were still part and parcel of Hitler's war machine. The Führer had previously told Eden that the Storm Troopers were a German version of the Salvation Army! Barthou of course considered the S.A. a part of the German Army.

Barthou once again told Simon that any future disarmament program to be considered must not endanger French security. Simon, appearing more concerned about Hitler's reactions, said that he was inclined to agree with the Führer's contention that his country should be allowed to have big guns and other heavy military equipment. Barthou asked Simon why it was necessary to grant the Germans their request since it had been clearly indicated that all heavy armaments would eventually be destroyed when an agreement had been reached. Simon could not give Barthou a logical answer. He continued to promise that France would receive the cooperation of his Government, but said Britain would not be a party to any action calling for the application of sanctions against Germany if she violated the Convention.

Simon's specious reasoning hardly justified his stance. If the Commission declared that a nation had violated its obligations, the agreement would be declared null and void. This, Simon said, "was a strong enough position. Germany must necessarily be more anxious than anybody else for the record period to begin when she would achieve equality with the other nations."

He tried to convince Barthou that "the gravity of the situation would affect His Majesty's Government as much as the French Government." And he assured the French statesman that there was no suggestion that either Government should disregard it or disassociate themselves from it . . . but he could not consider putting anything in the nature of new sanctions into the document.

On September 25, Simon, Baron von Neurath, Fulvio Suvich, the Deputy Foreign Minister of Italy, and his assistant Baron Pompeo Aloisi met to discuss the disarmament question. The Italians did not want to have any international commission checking up on Germany. It was their opinion that such a commission would tend to give security to France while equality was being denied to Germany during the first probationary period.

At first, Simon took a firm position toward the Germans and Italians. He told them that there was no possibility of Whitehall's granting the Germans equality in arms during the first period. In a letter to Prime Minister MacDonald after he had held his meeting with the two totalitarians, he wrote that the German attitude was not a "reasonable" one. But he did not hold fast to that opinion for very long. On October 6, the Germans, still refusing to submit to any probationary periods, demanded that the powers should agree on a five-year Convention, subdivided into stages. Insisting that they should be allowed to attain an equality in arms from the start of the Convention, they refused to give the Allies any information about the equipment of the substituted force, nor would they reveal any facts about the transformation of the Reichswehr until their antagonists had told them what to expect: Germany was even demanding to be presented with samples of all the latest military equipment!

Mussolini chose this time to tell the democratic leaders that Hitler was "quite irresponsible." And without pausing to take a deep breath he warned them that Hitler was not to be trifled with because he had no fear of the consequences.

The Duce was talking through two sides of his mouth. He tried out the role of reasonable mediator, but it didn't fit: he had already practically committed himself to Germany. But the British and even Barthou were still inclined to believe that he could be lured into the anti-Nazi camp.

In a speech in which he talked about Italy's relations with the other European powers, Mussolini said: "We do not see much prospect of improving our relationship with our neighbors beyond the mountains. Or at least not so long as they continue to wound us in our most sensitive part. The first condition for a policy of friendship, a friendship which would be crystallized in diplomatic protocols, would be the discontinuance of those reflections on the valor of those Italian soldiers who shed their blood in the wilderness of Macedonia. . . . Nevertheless, we who are strong now demand, for the last time, the possibility of an understanding."

The double-faced Duce, who had already hired assassins to murder the ruler of the people beyond the mountains, had the gall to talk about peaceful relations between Italy and the Yugoslavs. While the statesmen of Europe were debating whether to start an arms race or to disarm, Mussolini had already decided to dismember Yugoslavia and cast his lot with Hitler.

15 *Murder in Marseilles*

A vedette boat from the destroyer *Dubrovnik* with the King aboard was slowly approaching the Quai des Belges. It was 4:05 P.M. Dozens of reporters and press photographers buzzed around the dock. Barthou, the mayor of the city, and General Georges, the French Army Chief of Staff, stood in a semicircle nearby, waiting for the King to make an appearance. Cannon boomed out a salute while seaplanes flew overhead.

An old-fashioned automobile with solid rubber tires and a two-step running board was standing by to transport the monarch through the city. Foissac, a peasant-turned-gendarme, was at the wheel, complaining in a strong Provençal accent that the vehicle had seen better days.

"This car is more like a hearse than an automobile," he remarked to another officer. "It won't go more than twenty miles an hour and it is very old. Wouldn't it be better to use the Mayor's car? After all, it's not an ordinary man I'll be driving. It is the King of Yugoslavia."

"Don't worry about it, Foissac," his friend said. "You'll not be going more than five miles an hour. Just keep her in first and all will be well."

According to one newspaperman, the car had been used to transport thieves and high-priced prostitutes to jail. Was this a macabre joke, or an insult to the monarch?

Alexander, looking every inch the king, stepped out of the vedette. He wore an admiral's uniform, a two-cornered admiral's hat with gold braid, and a white collar and tie. A scarlet ribbon of the French Legion of Honor was draped across his breast.

A group of soldiers who had fought with him on the Salonika front came stiffly to attention. A squad of French marines cheered him to the echo as he walked slowly toward Barthou. The King was pale; the sea had been extremely rough and, having been seasick, he was still feeling the effects of the voyage.

Barthou and the other officials bowed as the King approached them. The Foreign Minister was gracious but extremely formal in his greeting. The orchestra played the national anthems of France and Yugoslavia. The huge crowd shouted "Vive Alexander! Vive Alexander!" There were a few scattered cries of "Down with Alexander," but they were drowned out by the volume of sound from the enthusiastic crowd.

As the Mayor of Marseilles led the King and his entourage to the waiting cars a very young girl in a Provençal costume stepped forward, curtsied, and gave the King a huge bunch of wild flowers. Alexander appeared touched by this gesture; a smile spread over his face.

The hood covering the top of the vehicle was pulled aside so that the people could see the monarch as he was driven through their city. General Georges sat on a collapsible seat just behind Barthou and Alexander.

The car did not move; someone gave the order for Foissac to start driving and it began to roll slowly at last. Colonel Poilet rode his horse to the left of the car, while Captain Vigoreux paced his steed to the right. Yevtich, the Yugoslav Foreign Minister, Pietri, and the Mayor of Marseilles were in the car right behind the one carrying the King.

There was another delay when the press photographers asked Foissac to stop while they snapped a few more pictures of the King and Barthou. The car began to move again at 4:15 P.M., right behind the trumpeters and the Garde Mobile. As it was driven slowly along the Cannebière the crowds shouted "*Vive le roi!*" Seaplanes buzzed overhead, so low they barely missed the roofs of the buildings. The car's engine created so great a din, Barthou could not hear when the King spoke to him.

The procession was about to pass the Bourse. General Georges stuck his head out of the window to see what had happened to the cavalry escort. The horsemen were galloping away, already far from the car. He looked again and noticed that the police had their backs to the crowds instead of facing them. He must have wondered what had happened to the motorcycle escort intended as protective covering for the King. They had lost themselves in the wilds of the city, and by the time they reached the Cannebière they might just as well have remained at home that day.

A man clad in a brown suit lurched out of the crowd and leaped onto the old-fashioned running board. Colonel Poilet saw him but, assuming he was a photojournalist, made no attempt to stop him. Céléstin Galy, a slow-thinking gendarme standing near the Bourse, saw the man as he was about to jump onto the car, but thought some Serbian peasant was trying to touch the King. Captain Vigoreux was too busy displaying his talents as a horseman to notice what was going on. Foissac did not see the man at first. But he did hear a revolver shot. He turned around and tried to push the assassin off the two-step running board, using one hand to drive the car and the other to cope with the killer. Barthou, who had realized what the man was up to before he began to fire at the King, flung his own body over that of the monarch in an effort to save him. It was a useless gesture: Alexander had received a fatal wound.

When General Georges looked at the assassin's ugly countenance, vicious expression, and cold eyes, he was badly frightened, knowing that he could not cope with the murderer. He pushed the car door open and leaped out into the street.

Alexander was lying at the right-hand corner of the car. Barthou, who had been wounded in the arm, was on his knees on the floor of the vehicle, groaning with pain. Célestin Galy, the gendarme, suddenly came to life. He rushed toward the car and tried to grab the assassin. The killer brushed his hand aside and shot Galy in the stomach. The policeman fell to the ground moaning in agony.

People in the immediate vicinity of the car were now aware that an assassin was on the loose. Their cheers turned to cries of rage. Foissac got out of the vehicle and began to tug at the killer's jacket; General Georges also tried to help subdue him. The assassin took careful aim, and pumped several bullets into the General's arms and torso.

Barthou, bleeding profusely, had managed to crawl through the door that General Georges had opened. Blood from a severed artery covered his clothes and splashed into the street.

Colonel Poilet meanwhile was still galloping his horse. It took a few more shots to make him come awake. He reached the killer's side and began to sabre him down.

Yevtich and General Dimitrievich got out of their car and ran toward the one that carried the King. Yevtich stepped into the vehicle, felt for the monarch's pulse, and immediately concluded that Alexander had been killed. In a later version of the tragic event, Dimitrievich said that Alexander had been alive when he reached his side, and that he had whispered, "Save Yugoslavia. Take care of the Queen." But at the time,

Bogoljub Yevtich simply said that the King had died before he or the General had reached his side.

Vlada, the assassin, was now mortally wounded. Kral should have thrown a bomb to help him make his getaway, but Kral was petrified. Vlada still had the strength to fire two more bullets in the direction of the crowd, hoping to galvanize his Ustacha partner into action. But it was to no avail: Kral slipped out of the milling mob and ran to a bus that was about to leave for Aix.

Vlada cursed Kral, and the police. Colonel Poilet hit him again and again with his sabre. Some women nearby began to scream "Kill the assassin!"—the murderer had fatally wounded two of their number in the crowd. A gendarme ran up to the killer and tore the magazine out of his hand, thinking it was the revolver. Another policeman reached Vlada's side and shot him in the head. The chauffeur apparently had more lives than the proverbial cat. The mob now surged forward to kick at his prone form; it took some time to control them. Other policemen stood guard over the car containing the body of the monarch. The protection they should have provided for the live Alexander was now being accorded to his corpse.

Yevtich still hovered over the body of his King. Colonel Pavlovich, the Court Chamberlain, was standing nearby, and helped put Alexander's body across two seats of the car. Yevtich, using a small penknife, tried to cut the King's collar, to help him breathe more easily if by chance he was still alive. The little knife was not strong enough to slit the cloth, but Yevtich kept slashing away until he was able to cut through the King's vest. When it was pried open, blood spurted out in torrents, covering Yevtich's face and clothes. His hands continued to search Alexander's body for wounds. Blood ran in small rivulets into the street. A faint smile still hovered over the King's face. Yevtich, now quite certain that his intimate friend the King was actually dead, was overtaken by grief.

Vlada the Chauffeur lay quite still upon the pavement. The

mob surged forward again, a few of the curious looking into the car. Flashbulbs were snapping: this was the big story of the year. Policemen ran here and there in a state of almost complete confusion. The chief of police finally ordered Foissac to get back into the driver's seat and start moving the vehicle. He honked the horn and set off at twenty miles an hour. Men and women in front of the car barely had time to jump out of the way. The unseeing eyes of the dead ruler looked at the passing scene. Thousands along the route who had no way of learning of the events were still shouting "*Vive le roi!*" as the car rolled by them on its way to the Prefecture.

When the car pulled up alongside police headquarters the body was taken out and carried to the office of the chief magistrate. There were a few physicians around who wanted to examine it, but this was not permitted. Dr. Assali, considered the best physician in Marseilles, was Chief Medical Officer for Colonial Troops. He arrived at the Prefecture after about half an hour, felt for the King's pulse, and muttered, "Life has ceased." He told his assistant, Dr. Raoul Olmer, to perform an autopsy. It was found that Alexander had received two wounds. One bullet had entered the chest, grazing the heart. Another had penetrated the abdomen. Olmer later testified in court: "We could only note that death came very fast."

Dr. Assali now hurried to the bedside of General Georges, whose wounds were very serious. One bullet had passed through the left breast and penetrated the abdominal wall. Other wounds had been inflicted on both of his arms. General Georges was a very lucky man; the one bullet which could have proved fatal had been deflected by a metal decoration he had received from the Serbian Government. The next five months were touch and go for the General, but Dr. Assali was able to restore him to health.

Barthou was in agony at the Hôtel Dieu. Though his wounds were not considered critical, he had lost a large amount of blood. Someone had tied a tourniquet around his wrist. It should have been tied above his elbow, but no one had the knowledge or the presence of mind to move it. The best anyone could do was to place him on a slightly tilted table, hoping to stem the flow of blood.

Dr. Bonnal was the first doctor to appear at the scene. He examined the Foreign Minister and noticed that the tourniquet had been tied at the wrong place. He called for assistance in the makeshift operating room, where Drs. Audier and Carralorder and Bemefous were now present. Bonnal administered some ethyl chloride and probed for the ruptured artery. He found it, and joined the ends together. Barthou was given a blood transfusion, but a hemorrhage developed, and despite the best efforts of the doctors, Barthou succumbed to his rather superficial wound. At 4:40 P.M. the statesman whispered, "I suffer terribly. I'm thirsty." And then he passed away.

Céléstin Galy, the police officer who had been wounded, was in great pain in a ward of a local hospital. Yolande Paris and Mme. Durbec, who had been wounded by the assassin, died. Vlada, his face smashed beyond recognition by the enraged mob, also died that same day. The Ustacha had succeeded beyond their wildest dreams.

Ante Pavelich now confidently waited for the Kingdom to fall apart. Croatia would become an independent nation, and he, Pavelich, unsuccessful lawyer, would become the Poglavnik. But the country held firm. There was no uprising. Even the Croats stood fast and were grief-stricken when they heard that Alexander had been murdered. Pavelich and his vicious henchmen had employed violent methods in their attempt to achieve their aims. They did not realize that Italy and her Duce were simply using them to obtain domination of the Balkans. They were only pawns in the big power game. The real villains in the plot were Italy and Hungary.

16 Belgrade Learns of the Murder

🮢🮢🮢🮢🮢🮢🮢🮢🮢🮢🮢🮢🮢🮢🮢🮢

The people of Yugoslavia were the last to hear what had happened in Marseilles. Their newspapers carried stories about the reception the King had received when he stepped ashore in the city. They recounted in detail what the King had said and done, and mentioned that Queen Marie had gone to Dijon where she was awaiting the monarch. But for quite a while, not a word was written about the murders.

Belgrade was a gay city that day. The people strolled on the Knez Mikhailova, main promenade of the town. Restaurants and cafes were teeming with young people. A few at home were listening to the radio. They were surprised when the station went off the air. They tried to tune in to other stations outside the city, but they too had stopped broadcasting. It was a rather disturbing development and the Yugoslavs did not know what to make of it. Stations all over the Continent were announcing that murder had taken place in Marseilles, but the people of Yugoslavia were kept in the dark about the catastrophe.

Even as important an official as General Zhivkovich did not find out immediately. He was about to leave his home for the theatre when his phone rang. He lifted the receiver and heard someone from the palace tell him that he should go at once to the office of the Minister of the Court. He telephoned Prince Paul, Alexander's cousin. Paul's voice trembled as he told the General, "The King is dead. . . . Come at once to the palace."

Prime Minister Uzunovich had received a telegram from Marseilles, reporting that the monarch was dead. For some reason he never explained, he refused to believe it. Mussolini's broadcasters were telling all who listened that the King had been murdered. The Prime Minister heard the broadcasts, but attributed the news to some deep plot aimed at creating chaos in the country. He, for one, was not going to believe anything the Fascists were saying. He ordered all the local radio stations shut down. The Prime Minister, all on his own, without consulting anyone, was going to save the nation from the Duce even if it meant cutting Yugoslavia off from the rest of the world.

At five o'clock the telephone rang. Uzunovich answered. It was Yevtich calling him from Marseilles. Uzunovich roared with laughter: it did not sound like Yevtich; it was probably an agent of Mussolini trying to confuse him. He listened further.

"I am speaking from the Prefecture at Marseilles," the voice said. "I am sorry to tell you that the King has been . . ."

Uzunovich did not let him finish the sentence. He slammed the receiver down. The telephone rang again; Uzunovich picked it up again. He was very angry. This business had gone far enough. He knew Yevtich. The voice was that of a stranger —he was certain of it. He slammed the phone down once more . . . and once more it rang. He snatched it up and without waiting to hear anything he shouted, "If you are Yevtich tell me your first name."

"Bogoljub," said the voice.

"I am not convinced that you are Yevtich," the Prime Minister said. "Anyone could find out the first name of our Foreign Minister. What is your wife's maiden name?"

The answer came.

"Yes, that is correct," Uzunovich said. "And what is your uncle's first name? . . . That is right. Well, my dear sir, you have obviously made quite a study of the Yevtich family, but I still do not believe you are the gentleman himself. I am becoming very impatient with you. You are taking up my time. And you are tying up my telephone. Get off the phone."

Yevtich was becoming frantic. How could he convince the Prime Minister that it was indeed he? He turned to General Dimitrievich and asked him to talk to Uzunovich. After that conversation Uzunovich ordered all the theatres and other public places shut down, and saw to it that there would be no special editions of the newspapers on the streets of Belgrade that night.

Prince Paul was in his palace while all this was going on. He was not an official of the Government, and had had no direct communication with Uzunovich or any other politician. His radio was out of order. He first learned what had happened in Marseilles when General Dimitrievich called him after talking to the Prime Minister. At first the General tried to lighten the blow. He told the Prince that the doctors were still trying to save the King. He phoned Paul a few minutes later and broke the true news that his cousin was dead.

Through a window, the Prince could see Alexander's palace across the street. He walked out into the dark avenue and ran swiftly toward the bleak-looking building. The guards allowed him to enter, and he hastened to the library. Alexander had told him of a will placed somewhere in the room. It was imperative that he find the document before the night was

over. He knew what it contained. In effect, he was to be the
acting ruler of the country until the heir to the throne would
come of age. The will would have to be shown to the Prime
Minister before he could take over the Government.

While Alexander had told Paul that the document was in
the library, he had neglected to specify where he had hidden
it. Paul looked through all the desk drawers. He looked
through all the cabinets, and thumbed through mountains of
files. He read countless letters. He found two large envelopes,
sealed with the royal coat of arms, between two volumes of
Molière on a bookshelf. One of the envelopes was addressed
to the President of the State Council, the other, to the Queen.
He put them back on the shelf and sent for General Zhivkovich
and two other army officers. He told them that the King's
documents were on the bookshelf and that he would not touch
them until Uzunovich had read them. He then called for the
Prime Minister.

Uzunovich, however, was playing a little game of his own.
Planning to take over the Government himself, he had already
been in touch with the Yugoslav Embassy officials in London,
and had requested that the young heir be returned to Yugoslavia. He had also ordered the deceased King's body transported back to his native land. It was Uzunovich's intention
to run the country and use the eleven-year-old Peter as a front.

But Prince Paul, fully aware of what the Prime Minister
had in mind for the country, sent an officer of the Royal Guard
to Uzunovich's office with instructions to produce him. When
Uzunovich entered the library, Paul told him where the envelopes could be found. The Prime Minister read the first
letter, which said that Paul was to become Regent in the event
of Alexander's death. The Prime Minister, Paul, and the army
officers then discussed what kind of a regency should be established in the Kingdom.

Meanwhile, messages from Marseilles were arriving in an
unending stream. One gave the details of the King's wounds.

Another stated that he had died before the doctors had examined him. A report came in that the assassin's name was Peter Keleman. It was followed by a description of how the killer had entered the country. The last telegram stated that Keleman had tried to kill himself but had been prevented by the police from doing so.

In a lengthy telephone conversation with an important Paris official, Paul was informed that the Queen had been told by the Prefect of Police of Dijon that the King had been murdered. He also learned that special editions of the newspapers were on the streets of many French cities with stories about the King's dedication to the cause of peace, quoting him as saying that Yugoslavia must remain a friend of France.

Rumors circulated. There was an air of consternation in Paris. The Cabinet was in session. General Georges was dead. (That rumor was not true.) The newspapers were preparing an appeal that King Alexander, as the peacemaker of Europe, should be awarded the Nobel Peace Prize. The President of the Republic, M. Lebrun, had sent the Prime Minister of Yugoslavia his warmest sympathy. The Yugoslav Ambassador to Vienna telephoned that the Austrian newspapers were printing sensational stories about a revolution in Yugoslavia.

News—both true and false—continued to pour into the palace. If one were to believe the journalists, the Government had closed all roads leading from Austria into Yugoslavia. The Queen, one report had it, had learned that her husband was going to be killed while she was traveling through Italy. Prince, now King, Peter was at last recalled from London.

Things moved swiftly that night. Italy's Fascists still expected that the country would be torn apart. The men in the palace library held the fate of the nation in their hands. The members of the Cabinet were summoned and asked to take an oath of allegiance to the young King. The army and navy officers took the same oath. An announcement was issued informing the people that for the time being, King Peter II would not actually reign. Prince Paul ordered that black-bordered flags be flown from all government buildings.

When the citizens of Belgrade awoke the next morning they read a proclamation on the black-bordered front page of *Vreme:*

To the People of Yugoslavia—

Our great King Alexander has fallen victim to a treacherous attempt on his life on October 9th at 4 P.M. at Marseilles.

With blood the King Martyr sealed that work of peace on which he was engaged in allied France.

To the throne of Yugoslavia succeeds his first-born son, His Majesty Peter II . . . God Save the King.

The people were stunned. All was quiet on the streets of the capital and the other major cities of the country. There were no demonstrations. The Croats too mourned the death of their monarch. Many of them were afraid the Serbs would hold them responsible for the murder. Early messages from Paris had indicated that the assassin had been a Croat. This was not true, of course. There was nothing to fear from the Serbs. They were in no mood to revenge themselves on their countrymen.

The identity of the murderer was pinpointed after a Serbian newspaperman received permission from the French police to examine the killer's body. After noticing the letters I.M.R.O. tattooed on Vlada's arms, the reporter knew he beheld a Bulgarian, not a Croat—and actually recognized who he was.

The Yugoslav Government was informed that the assassin had been identified, but decided not to publicize the fact that he was a Bulgarian. The people might become incensed and create a public outcry to declare war against a country with whom Yugoslavia had established cordial relations.

Many sympathetic messages from heads of state and prominent art and literary figures poured into Belgrade. Adolf Hitler, no friend of the dead King, expressed his horror at the deed. The master of doubletalk, Benito Mussolini, who had been providing funds to the Ustacha for the very purpose, assured Prince Paul that "the tragic decease of the exalted monarch of Yugoslavia as the victim of such a dastardly attempt has evoked the keen indignation of the Italian nation which shares the feeling of sorrow of the Yugoslav nation. Pray accept (my) expression of the most lively and profound sympathy of the Fascist power and of myself personally."

The Austrian and Hungarian leaders also expressed deep sorrow, once more proving the wisdom of the man who said that politics is a whore's business.

17 The Ustacha Who Lost His Nerve

ᄀᄀᄀᄀᄀᄀᄀᄀᄀᄀᄀᄀᄀᄀᄀᄀᄀᄀᄀᄀ

Mio Kral had stood frozen in his tracks while Vlada the Chauffeur pumped bullets into the King, Barthou, General Georges, Galy, and two innocent bystanders. But he suddenly found that he had feet and that they could carry him to safety.

Kral took the omnibus to Aix. The bus driver did not know what had happened; Kral looked like just another passenger to him. The Ustacha's arrival in Aix was not noticed. He walked to the hotel and wandered about the lobby. After a few minutes he went into the hotel restaurant. When the waiter asked for his order, Kral said he was waiting for a friend and would order when he arrived. Extremely nervous, he smoked one cigarette after another. He was afraid Pavelich would learn that he had not tossed the bombs into the crowd as he had been told to do, and have him killed.

After an hour Kral left the restaurant and went to his room.

He ripped the mattress apart as he had seen Maria do, placed the bombs, revolvers, and ammunition among the springs, and then sewed it together again. But he would have been wiser if he had thrown the weapons into the river. Kral was a very stupid man.

He should not, of course, have remained in the hotel. Once the police learned what had occurred in Marseilles, they would check into every room and probably find him. But Kral expected an Ustacha to come to Aix looking for Pospishil. That contact would help Kral get out of France—or at least he hoped it would. Kral had been told to travel to Switzerland via Avignon, Paris, and Fontainebleau, thence to Thonon and on by boat to the other side of Lake Geneva. From that point he was to use his compass and go due east over the Alps to Italy.

Kral was in too confused a state to remember the instructions he had received from the Ustacha.

At seven in the evening a local man, arriving home from a trip to Marseilles, ran into Kral's hotel and shouted that the King of Yugoslavia had been murdered. The local people did not believe him. At that moment another man ran into the hotel lobby waving a copy of *Le Matin*. There on the front page was the complete story of the assassination.

Kral, losing control of himself, ran from the lobby out into the street and hailed a taxicab, shouting "Take me to Avignon." The driver looked at him; a passenger would have to be supplied with plenty of money to afford *that* fare. The man looked like a criminal. But it was no business of his to worry about a customer's profession. He drove to Avignon.

The Ustacha had told Kral to stop at a certain sidestreet. He handed the cab driver two hundred francs and received some change, which he did not even stop to count. He walked to the railroad station, where he paced back and forth in a nervous frenzy. He bought a ticket for Paris. He boarded the train and walked along the corridor until he found an empty compartment, where he stretched out in a berth. His nerves felt like live electric wires; he couldn't sleep. Was Vlada still alive? Would he tell Pavelich how his partner had failed him? Would Pavelich forgive him for deserting Vlada?

Pavelich had named the Café de la Paix as the rendezvous after the assassination. There would probably be a Pavelich deputy there to tell him what to do now.

Kral's train arrived at the Gare de Lyon early in the morning. He looked around, but no one seemed to be following him. He could not read French, but he could make out what was happening by looking at the pictures in the newspaper he bought. There was one photograph of the still-living killer, and another taken after the mob had trampled him. Vlada was dead. That was a relief. Now Pavelich would not learn what had happened.

Kral began to feel somewhat better. He took a bus to the Café de la Paix and sat down at a street table. He ordered brioches and café au lait, and drank several cups. He was all alone. He began to panic again. He looked in vain for an Ustacha, but none appeared. He had better leave Paris! His friends Pospishil and Raich were probably in Fontainebleau; they would help him. He asked for the bill, handed the waiter some money, and walked to the street corner. The bus to the Place d'Italia would put him where he could get another bus for Fontainebleau. But the bus did not come, so he hailed a taxi. The cab driver discharged him at the Fontainebleau railroad station—and then notified the police that there was a very suspicious-looking character in town. Kral looked all over the city for his friends, while the Fontainebleau police wired Paris. The Paris police wired back that the foreigner should be picked up: three detectives had been dispatched to arrest him. Kral went back to the railroad station, and found the police waiting for him.

They examined his passport, issued in the name of Maly. The photograph looked like him. Not satisfied, the police had begun to search him when he suddenly bolted and disappeared into the forest at the edge of town.

The night was very cold. Kral had to sleep on the ground, as there was no shelter to be found. He was in the forest for the next twenty-four hours. After nightfall, he ventured outside the wood and walked on the road toward Paris. He looked in vain for a roadhouse where he could get some food. He was very tired and hungry. Lost, he wandered around in circles for the next three days. On the fourth day, he found a road just outside the forest. He lay down in a ditch and fell asleep.

On the fifth day he walked on the open road. He had now been without food for six days. Guideposts indicated that he was on the main road to Paris. If he could only manage to get to the capital, he would be able to find help. He still had seven hundred francs in his pocket, enough to carry him for awhile.

On October 5, the local police in Melun received a telegram that a foreigner had been observed at a bar near Corbeil, paying two francs, fifty centimes for a cup of coffee. The price was only sixty centimes, and the average Frenchman was not that extravagant. The bar owner had become suspicious, and he notified the police, who arrived about fifteen minutes after Kral had left the place. They caught up with him as he was trudging along the road toward Paris. He did not want to discuss the murders. Food was the only thing on his mind, and he wanted to know if the police would feed him. Told that they would, he promised to give them all the information they wanted.

While Kral wandered in the woods near Fontainebleau, Pospishil and Raich had attempted to cross the border into Switzerland. They didn't make it: the police apprehended the pair just as they were about to step onto Swiss soil.

Vlada the Chauffeur had been identified. Pavelich and Kvaternik had made good their escape from France to Italy. The Italians picked the pair up in Turin and hid them on an island off the coast. Mussolini was determined to keep the two Ustacha out of the hands of the French police. If they were extradited, they would talk, and reveal his own complicity in the murders.

18 The Funeral in Paris, and the Whitewash in Geneva

The funeral of Louis Barthou took place on October 13, a bleak autumn day. All the shops in the French capital were closed. Flags on public buildings were covered with black bunting and flew at half mast. Black-bordered posters had been plastered on the walls of buildings in all the arrondissements. The people learned that Barthou was going to have "a national funeral."

The cortege started from the Quai d'Orsay, which was draped in black. Republican Guards led the solemn procession. Open carriages with wreaths presented by various veterans' organizations were right behind the Guards. Next in line was the caisson with the coffin draped with the Tricolor. Barthou's family were in the carriage right behind the caisson, and following them were President Lebrun and Gaston Doumergue. Other carriages in the cortege bore distinguished men from foreign countries.

Premier Doumergue delivered a very moving speech in which he reminded his countrymen that it was Barthou who had convinced the national deputies to vote in favor of the three-year conscription act back in 1913, and that the additional manpower in the armed forces had enabled France to stop the German invasion at the Marne. "The patriotism which filled Barthou in those anxious hours," he said, "must be an example for the young generation."

Laval, who would destroy everything that Barthou had accomplished in the field of foreign relations, also spoke. "On the tablets of *patrie* where the names of Clemenceau, Foch, Briand, Dounet and Poincaré are inscribed, parliament would do well to write the name of Louis Barthou, who was worthy of being saluted from century to century by a grateful nation."

A Mass was offered at the Church of St. Louis des Invalides. The martyred leader was laid to rest in the cemetery of Père Lachaise where so many of France's greatest sons are buried.

Many of the world's leaders rose that day to express their sorrow at the untimely demise of the French statesman. Anthony Eden, whose Government had given Barthou so many difficult moments, extended his sympathies. Goering, who was also there, was more honest. He told Ward Price, the correspondent for the London *Daily Mail* (who was an admirer of Hitler), that he hoped Barthou's policies were buried with him.

In his memoirs, Anthony Eden wrote that Barthou had "learned that Anglo-French cooperation had to be. . . . He had vigor enough to make such cooperation real. He was not mean in friendship nor in ambition, and, at the close of the League Assembly a few weeks earlier, I could describe Anglo-French relations as better, essentially franker than I have ever known them. His policy was direct and disinterested depending on the personal enthusiasm with which he alone could back it. I could see no obvious successor, certainly none of his stature. I bitterly regretted losing a man who had, I thought, become a friend. To this day I value the copy he gave me of his Life of Mirabeau with the inscription which, from a man of his experience, generously flattered my years. For France the day was fateful. At no time after this did she have so courageous and forceful a statesman to serve as Foreign Minister. Intrigue there was, and sincere devotion, but until the war engulfed all five years later, never inspired direction and the blunt speech which might have warned Rome, for instance, while there was still time."

Eden always believed that the shots that killed Barthou and King Alexander were "the first shots of the Second World War."

But the man who became Prime Minister never explained why his Government continued to appease Hitler and displayed so little confidence in Barthou. Nor did he ever record that Barthou had thrown him a Nazi salute as he entered the League of Nations Assembly Hall at the last session of that august body. Barthou was obviously telling Eden that his policies and those of his Government were gratifying to the men in Berlin. But Eden chose to forget that incident.

❖   ❖   ❖   ❖

Murder had been committed in Marseilles and now it was deemed necessary to get Mussolini off the hook. If the Yugoslavs had any thought of implicating Italy in the plot, Laval and Eden were equally determined that they would have none of that. Eden was assigned the thankless task of cooling the tempers of the Yugoslavs and keeping the Italians satisfied that they would be given a whitewash. Eden's superior, Sir John Simon, delegated him to keep the situation under control.

The leaders of the Little Entente who were in Geneva held a conference and discussed what tactics they should adopt at the upcoming debates. Titulescu chaired the conclave. Greek and Turkish representatives also participated.

After very involved discussion, the mountain gave birth to a little mouse. The diplomats discovered that a double murder had been "committed under the influence of forces beyond the frontiers." No one thought of mentioning what frontiers they were referring to.

Further reflection brought forth the suggestion that "all states without exception should cooperate in a tranquil and objective spirit to establish the guilty parties."

But the spirit of tranquility vanished when Laval and his British helper started to pressure the smaller nations to abstain from accusing Italy of the crime.

Benes of Czechoslovakia told Eden that public opinion in Belgrade was demanding that the terrorists should be expelled from Italy and Hungary and an international convention assembled to deal with the Ustacha and the I.M.R.O. But Eden, still acting under the instructions of his Government, refused to take that suggestion seriously. He told Benes that he was gravely concerned about the effects of a prolonged and acrimonious debate on future relations among Italy, Britain, and France. He also thought there was some justification for Italy's sympathetic attitude toward Hungary, since that nation was being accused of having provided a haven for the terrorists.

Benes did not agree with Eden, but he promised to do all he could to hold the debate from getting out of control. He warned Eden that the Yugoslavs were thoroughly aroused, and demanding that the guilty should be punished. Something would have to be done, he said, to appease Belgrade.

On November 21, Yevtich told Eden that his Government was about to circulate a memorandum accusing Hungary of having been one of the parties to the murders. His delegation, he said, had taken special pains to keep Italy out of the picture, even though they knew Mussolini's Fascists had been involved in the outrage. The Yugoslavs had compiled a vast amount of facts about Hungary's criminal activities. The document ran to 150 pages, folio size. It detailed the actions of the Budapest authorities, and contained a record of all the crimes that the Ustacha and the I.M.R.O. had committed. It also showed proof that there was a connection between CZAR (the French Rightist organization) and the Ustacha, and it mentioned many aspects of Italy's role in terrorism apart from the assassinations then being discussed.

Eden tried to be sympathetic. He was willing to cooperate with the Yugoslavs provided they did not involve Italy in the mess. He expressed great concern for Yevtich's future as a politician and promised that he would try to cast some of the blame on at least one of the culprits. Hungary was being picked to serve as the scapegoat by the two major powers.

Pierre Laval suddenly made an appearance in Geneva, his arrival astonishing everyone. Laval was worried about what was going on in Geneva. Those wild Yugoslavs were a very unpredictable people and there was no telling what they were likely to do if he wasn't around to control them. If they accused Italy of the crime, it would spoil all his plans to come to a good understanding with Mussolini. He told Eden that France would withdraw her military support from Yugoslavia if Yevtich persisted in maligning poor Mussolini. He, Laval, had been told that the Yugoslavs had released a detailed memorandum in which they named Italy as one of the chief instigators of the Ustacha. He intended to talk tough to Yevtich.

Eden continued to maintain his pose as an honest broker, whose sole purpose was to prevent a world war from breaking out. But there was another good reason for protecting Italy's good name: he wanted to keep Mussolini from making a final commitment to Hitler. The Duce, to be sure, wanted Italy to become the dominant power in Southern Europe, the Mediterranean Sea, Mare Nostrum. How that could reconcile with British need for control of that vital waterway was something to which Eden and his Government had not given much creative thought.

Before he left home for Geneva, Eden had told Charles Corbin, the French Ambassador to London, that he hoped to have the upcoming debate at the League postponed for several months, to give passions time to cool. But when he got to the Swiss city, he realized that a delay would only intensify the crisis. He decided to call for an immediate meeting of the League's Council.

A special committee of the League was called into session. Its chairman was Senhor Vasconcellos, a Portuguese diplomat selected by the British because Portugal was an ally and danced to Britain's tune in matters pertaining to foreign policy. Vasconcellos could be relied upon to follow Eden's instructions to the letter.

Mussolini was becoming alarmed, and afraid of a war. His army was too weak to stand up against the Yugoslavs. Threats shouted from the balcony of the Palazzo Venezia were one thing: he could impress his excitable audience. But he knew, better than most, that a conflict would spell the doom of his regime. He told his good friend Sir Eric Drummond that he expected England to exercise a restraining influence on the Yugoslavs.

The general debate began on December 7. By then Laval had had enough time to intimidate Yevtich and force his promise to confine himself to some minor accusations against the Hungarians. Tibor von Eckhardt, the spokesman for the Hungarians, kept insisting that his country was innocent of any wrong-doing. Hungary knew nothing about the Ustacha nor did she engage in the criminal activities of which the Yugoslavs were accusing her.

The Council session went off quite well—for Eden. Laval pretended to stand up for his good friends the Yugoslavs. Baron Aloisi, the Italian diplomat, soothed the Hungarians and promised that Italy would support them. Eden, still per- plexed and well-meaning, only wishing to see that justice was done, declared that he found it very difficult to arrive at any decision about placing the responsibility for the murder on any one nation. The proceedings were still subjustice in France where the murders had been committed. Eden suggested that the discussions in Geneva should proceed with extreme caution.

The South American diplomats criticized Eden's behavior. Benes, Titulescu, and Yevtich were fit to be tied. Salvador de Madariaga, representing Spain at the League, found the actions of the major powers odious.

The next Council meeting was scheduled for the following Monday. Over the weekend, many of the most important European newspapers were very critical of Eden and Laval. One French paper called Eden a modern Pontius Pilate.

While Yevtich was trying to stand firm against the combined pressure of Laval and Eden, he was being undermined at home by the crafty Uzunovich, whose journalistic minions were asking many embarrassing questions. They accused Yevtich of selling out his country, and denounced the delegation memorandum as weak and without any substance. The Prime Minister did not tell his people that Yevtich was being terrorized by the insidious Laval. Yugoslavia wanted to know why Italy had not been accused of the murder, and why the case against Hungary was so flimsy. Uzunovich, to whom Yevtich was a dangerous political opponent, trained all his propaganda guns on the Foreign Minister. Some of the facts he cited against Yevtich were true, but half-truths do not make a whole story.

Yevtich tried to fight against the Lavals and the Edens, to tear aside the veil that was obscuring the truth. But the fast footwork of his so-called friends in the democratic West prevented him from exposing the criminals. He was further embarrassed when Uzunovich suddenly started expelling hundreds of harmless Hungarian farmers from Yugoslavia. The European press published pictures of the refugees, many of whom were old and feeble, or children. Stories about these suffering people created an antagonistic feeling against the Yugoslavs among other European peoples.

Eden knew that Yevtich had had nothing to do with the expulsions, but that did not stop him from delivering a speech on December 8 in which he accused the Belgrade Government of using the murder of the King to justify its treatment of helpless farmers. The vehemence that Eden displayed that day impressed some Council members. But the cynics among them took note that he had not shown so much emotion about the murderous actions of the pawns of the Italian and Hungarian governments.

Yevtich could not accept the accusations with good humor. What kind of a man could expect him to take that kind of abuse from his so-called friends? He told his associates to get ready to leave Geneva. In Titulescu's hotel room he told Benes and the other leaders of the Little Entente that he was leaving because his nation had been grossly insulted by Eden and Laval. He warned them that Yugoslavia would probably leave the League. How could anyone expect her to remain a member when the democracies were in cahoots with the two countries that had supported the Ustacha?

Benes and Titulescu advised him to stay on—any withdrawal of that kind might start a war. But Yevtich was not to be persuaded by their arguments. He promised only to discuss his impending departure with Pierre Laval. What did he hope to gain from a discussion with that slippery individual? Laval had no intention of casting Italy into the limelight as a sponsor of assassins.

The little lawyer from the Auvergne received Yevtich with a smile, and assured him that Eden's remarks were of no importance. He, Laval, intended to give a speech which would prove how good a friend he was of Yugoslavia. "France is with you," the tricky counselor swore. "France is devoted to Yugoslavia and our interests are united. On Monday, when I speak, you will learn that I have 'become a Yugoslav.'"

There could be very little comfort in all of this for Yevtich: lo and behold, Laval reverted immediately to his original structure; France would support Yugoslavia if she did not press any charges against Italy. Yevtich threatened outright to leave

Geneva. Laval became very nervous: the wild Yugoslav would spoil all his plans. He asked Yevtich to delay leaving until he had discussed the Yugoslav case with the members of the Council. What were Yevtich's minimum demands? Could he come up with a formula? "The British love formulas," he said. "Feed them formulas and you will have them eating out of your hand."

Poor Yevtich, unaware of how completely he was being manipulated by Laval, returned to his hotel and wrote a statement outlining his minimum conditions. When Laval read it the next morning, he insisted on making some changes, for Yevtich was still accusing Italy of being behind the murders, and that was no more acceptable than it had been before. As he was rewriting the statement, Laval told Yevtich that Italy would stand before the bar of public opinion at a later date. This was not the time to force the issue, he said as he advised Yevtich to concentrate on the Hungarians. The turn for the Italians would come soon enough. Yevtich set aside his misgivings, but obviously he did not know Laval very well.

It was now important to have Eden's seal of approval of the new statement as concocted by Laval. But the Frenchman could not locate the Britisher, off playing golf somewhere. Laval had no notion of letting the Yugoslav off his well-baited hook. While he waited for Eden he would have a talk with Baron Pompeo Aloisi and get him to approve the statement.

Aloisi balked at first, but Laval was able to swing him around by assuring him that Italy would not be put on the spit. So long as the good name of his nation would not be tarnished by any Yugoslav, Aloisi agreed to abide by the Laval formula. Hungary would be told to accept the role of the guilty party.

Von Eckhardt and Kanya, the next two with whom Laval discussed the matter, did not like the idea of their country being pilloried with the eyes of the world looking at her discomfiture. They haggled back and forth, finally agreeing that

Hungary could accept the blame for some minor infractions of international law. A number of very obscure officials would be blamed for encouraging the Ustacha to stage their raids into Yugoslavia, but the Government would be absolved completely.

Laval had won his battle. He told Eden that Yevtich and the Belgrade Government had capitulated to his demands. Eden decided that the British should guide the Council toward the plan of the two major powers. After talking to Sir John Simon he had another talk with Laval. Von Eckhardt was still telling the League Council that Yanka Pusta was a home for innocent refugees who had fled from the terror in their own country. Ironically enough, it was Maurice Nègre, a French journalist, who had first discovered the terrorist encampment and had revealed his findings to the world.

After a great deal of hemming and hawing, the Council issued the statement of its decision. And what a decision it was! The Council admitted that terrorist activity had been encouraged by Hungary. Italy was not mentioned at all. Those activities had not yet been stopped, and the Yugoslav Government had good cause to be concerned about them. The Council held some minor Hungarian officials responsible for the continued terrorism, and for the murders in Marseilles, but it expressed its confidence in the good will of the Hungarian Government and declared that that Government could be expected to cooperate with the League to put an end to the condition. It requested that Budapest keep the Council informed of its progress in that direction.

But that was not quite all. A committee was to be organized to make a study of terrorism and arrive at a solution to the grave problem. The men who would be selected to form the committee would represent a number of powers. Some of them would be citizens of Hungary and Italy.

In a gesture of appeasement toward the Yugoslavs, the Council condemned the heinous crime that had been perpe-

trated in Marseilles, and ordered that all those who had participated in the outrage should be made to pay for their deeds.

By this time even Yevtich knew that he had been taken in
by Laval and Eden. The Yugoslav people were very unhappy
at the turn of events. But London and Budapest were pleased,
and Laval was quite satisfied with what he had achieved. He
had, or so he thought, convinced Mussolini that France was a
good friend of Italy . . . an investment that could be expected
to pay good dividends in the future.

In the end, however, the biggest losers were Britain and
France. The pro-French and pro-British politicians of Yugo-
slavia lost all faith in the promises of the two democracies.
The pro-German Milan Stoyadinovich became Premier after
Yevtich was deposed after a brief stay in office. The Regent,
Prince Paul, began to advocate a friendlier attitude toward
Berlin. But the people of Yugoslavia still looked to the democratic West for guidance. When their pro-German leaders
swung the country into the Axis camp some years later, the
people staged an uprising and allied themselves with the
French and the British. Laval, as was to be expected, became
a Nazi collaborator when war finally broke out on the Continent.

19   *The Trial*

The first trial of the Ustacha assassins took place in Aix-en-Provence during November 1935. Various influences had been brought into play to delay the trial; some very important men in France and elsewhere tried to keep it from taking place at all. But public opinion was strong and it demanded that the culprits be punished. Then too there was the League Council statement calling for the criminals to be tried. Laval was still intent on keeping certain facts from being exposed. All the Yugoslavs wanted was for the truth to be revealed. Laval was confident that the trial could be controlled by him. The people might cry for vengeance but Yevtich had fallen by the wayside—or been kicked aside—and Stoyadinovich was now in charge. Laval had been busily engaged in digging a pit for others, and was now succeeding in undermining the French alliance in Eastern Europe. With that bulwark destroyed, the Balkans would move into the German-Italian orbit.

The farce began. The real criminals, the Ustacha leaders, were safely hidden away in Italy. The president of the court looked very dignified as he ordered the trial to start. Before the lawyers began their wrangling, he asked all to stand and pay their respects to the martyred Alexander, the hero who had fought against the enemies of France during the Great War. He also asked the journalists, lawyers, court attendants and spectators to pay homage to that "apostle of the amity of the peoples, Louis Barthou."

Monsieur Desbons, the lawyer for the defendants, was a very emotional individual who insisted that the spectators should remain standing and bow their heads to honor the poor persecuted Croats and Macedonians who had laid down their lives to win freedom for their countries.

The president of the court picked a number of men to serve as interpreters. Desbons raised the objection that all of them were Serbs, and one had tortured the defendants in prison. The court had not been able to find one Frenchman who could speak the Serbian language. All the interpreters were natives of Yugoslavia who knew their own tongue but had only a smattering of French at their disposal. Desbons made a hysterical speech in which he accused the court of having prejudged his clients. The interpreters, he said, were in the pay of Belgrade, and he refused to recognize them. The president of the court roared out that the hearing would continue "whether they accept or not."

During the afternoon session Desbons said that the president's ruling was illegal. At that point the procurator-general demanded that Desbons be disciplined, declaring that he had never witnessed such behavior by a lawyer in any French court. Desbons, however, was not to be silenced. He orated for the next hour and made no sense at all.

Kral, Pospishil, and Raich were all but forgotten. The trial was now completely dominated by the verbal battles be-

tween Desbons and the court officials. All the while, the three
defendants were having a conversation among themselves.
Desbons once took the witness stand himself, to assert that his
honor was being impugned by the president of the court and
his procurator-general. Holding his hand to his heart and with
tears streaming down his face, he cried out to the whole
courtroom and the world.

"You can punish me if you wish, but when you have punished me there will remain a joy which you will not be able
to take from me, that, in receiving your sentence, I shall be
conscious of having accomplished to the full my sacred mission which is that of a defending counsel. The sentence you
. . . will pronounce against me today, will have no other result
than to make me adore this gown which up to now I have
only loved."

A recess was called. The president of the court, the procurator-general, and a number of other legal dignitaries discussed Desbons for several hours. They finally decided that
he should be penalized with an official censure.

M. Casteran, a French journalist who had worked as an
accredited correspondent in Belgrade, was now asked to serve
as interpreter. But he was a very busy man and could only
give the court one afternoon a week, hardly enough. On the
following day a Yugoslav Moslem was asked to fill in. Pospishil
suddenly came to life and protested the use of the Moslem.
Then Desbons took over and started to read a very long report
that had been issued by the League of Nations Council. The
president of the court ordered him to stop. Desbons remained
silent while the court called a number of medical authorities
to give evidence that Kral was unbalanced. The lawyers for
the defense claimed (though it was not true) that the prison
authorities had attempted to hypnotize him. The medical men
insisted that Kral was a victim of his own hallucinations. The
president of the court listened patiently as the learned doctors

talked about the difference between an ordinary hallucination and a neurosis. The discussion had no bearing on the crime of which the Ustacha were accused.

One of the more prestigious doctors, a staff member of the Toulouse Insane Asylum, said that Kral was suffering from "a slight attenuation of responsibility." Dr. Digue, in a different approach, told the court that he had had a number of sessions with the prisoner and had then submitted his findings to a group of eminent medical specialists in practical psychology. It was their opinion that the defendant Kral did have hallucinations and that he was a neurotic who could be easily influenced by a stronger mind to commit a crime. He could be made to believe that the idea had originated in his own mind. Dr. Digue concluded by saying that Kral could not be held responsible for the murder, and that he should not be sentenced to death.

Dr. Euzière had come to the same conclusions. He had detected some telltale signs that Kral had intermittent or delirious hallucinations, and that he also had some kind of vascular disease that prevented the free circulation of blood through his body.

Professor Corneille was then called to give his opinion. Desbons started to argue with him for no apparent reason. The professor and Desbons discussed Kral's symptoms, which Corneille felt were not very important. Desbons insisted that his client's reflexes were not in good working order. This medical debate was interrupted by the presiding judge. An usher gave him a note which he read and then destroyed. Desbons said that the note should have been read. The next half hour was taken up by a dispute between the lawyer and the presiding judge. Desbons called for a mistrial.

The presiding judge acknowledged that he had made a mistake. But Desbons would not accept his excuse. He hinted that evidence had been suppressed and that he, for one, had already concluded that it was impossible for his clients to be fairly tried in France. He cried out that the court would not "have the heads of these three men, neither you nor your substitute, the executioner.

"That," he thundered, "is justice for you. That's Republican justice."

He called again for a mistrial and even had the audacity to ask for the release of the three prisoners.

The trial was over. Even if the defendants were found guilty, there would be a demand to waive the verdict because of irregularities in procedure. The presiding judge was determined to ask for the disbarment of the obstructionist Desbons.

The fiery lawyer had no intention of apologizing for his outrageous behavior. He defended his actions by saying that his father had instilled in him a love of justice, and that he had always defended the helpless, and because he had always stood up for the lowly he was about to be destroyed.

The president of the court remained calm under the onslaughts of Desbons. He recounted the offenses the lawyer had committed during the trial: He had been in contempt of court; he had been an obstructionist; he had implied that the judge was not impartial; he had failed to abide by the rulings of the court; he had conducted himself in an unworthy manner. The court ruled that Desbons was guilty as charged. When the president of the court asked him to leave the bar, Desbons said, "I will not leave the bar unless expelled by military force."

The presiding judge motioned to a gendarme, indicating that he wanted to have Desbons removed. The lawyer was led away still shouting that his clients were innocent of any wrong-doing.

Desbons did not intend to remain quiet, and the next day was a very busy one for him. He called a press conference and told the reporters that he had been offered 400,000 francs by a mystery man if he would consent to ask certain questions during the pre-hearing of the trial. Certain powerful men, he said, were determined to create a climate of fear all over the Continent, hoping to lead France into a war. A number of highly placed Government figures had known about the plot to assassinate King Alexander. Desbons asked why the King had been invited to come to France. Was there a plot to have him killed? According to the lawyer the real truth about the assassinations would never be revealed. His own investigations had alarmed some important political luminaries, and were the real reason he had been disbarred. He had known that he would be persecuted before he had accepted the case.

Desbons made some very wild accusations, but he never really said anything. He never revealed who the mystery man was who had tried to bribe him, nor did he tell the journalists who was trying to spread fear throughout Europe. It was true that certain facts about the murder had been kept from the public. It was also known that a very large sum of money had been provided for the defendants to pay their lawyers. But Desbons wouldn't tell the newspapers who was paying for his services.

The trial was over; it had been more a brawl than a trial. Desbons was making a valiant attempt to confuse the public when he spoke about men trying to subvert justice. He never dared mention that Pierre Laval was the one who attempted all along to protect the speckled reputation of Benito Mussolini.

The entire world was waiting for some startling revelations, but they were doomed to be disappointed. The Yugoslavs learned that their monarch had not received adequate police protection. They also discovered, as many Frenchmen did, that a great statesman had been allowed to bleed unattended on the streets of a great city. And they as well as other decent Europeans wanted to know why this had been allowed to happen. The assassinations were committed in 1934. Thirty years later, the French Government still would not allow any researchers to examine the officials records of the case.

20 *The Second Trial*

The second trial of the Ustacha terrorists took place in the Department of Bouce du Rhône sixteen months after the murders were committed in Marseilles. M. Loison was now acting as the presiding judge, and M. Saint-Auban was the counsel for the defense.

It was a strange kind of trial, and in certain respects even more grotesque than the first one. George London, covering the trial for an English newspaper, made special note of the fact that the defendants were elegantly dressed. Someone was paying for their expensive clothes.

The Ustacha still took an antagonistic attitude toward the judge and the prosecutor. They told everyone within earshot that the trial was one huge joke.

The three terrorists guffawed as the first prosecution witness—a Yugoslav Officer of the Legion of Honor—gave his testimony. Saint-Auban harassed him during his entire period on the stand. The witness, undisturbed by anyone's antics, said that Colonel Perchets and Ante Pavelich had been supported by the Fascist Government and that Rome had ordered the Ustacha to commit the murders.

When the defendants were requested to take the witness stand they refused to leave their seats. Accusing the authorities of mistreating them during the first trial, they announced that Saint-Auban had been pressed upon them, and insisted on having Desbons represent them in court. When the presiding judge berated them for their shocking behavior, they accused the police of torturing them during an interrogation, and forcing them to sign certain statements. Kral, who had been called an unbalanced man at the first trial, now spoke up and said that a Serbian secret agent had promised him his freedom if he would agree to kill Ante Pavelich. Pospishil and Raich also said that the police had threatened to murder all their relatives in Yugoslavia if they did not confess to the crime.

The defendant Pospishil/Nowak, the most intelligent of the three Ustacha on trial and also the most dangerous of the group, refused to say anything at first. But Benes-alias-Raich talked too much for his own good.

"I am really Raich," he admitted. "I was born on January 5, 1913, in the town of Kokeiwitz in Croatia. I married Maria Kramer and my son is twelve years old. I am a member of Pavelich's organization. On September 28, I received orders to go to Munich where I met an unknown individual at the Cafe Deutscher Kaiser. He was a member of our secret organization. From this man I received money and false passports, and returned to Zurich."

Later on, Raich's testimony was corroborated by Police Commissioner Petit, who said that Raich had gone to Munich and had returned to Switzerland. No entry imprint had been found on Raich's passport, indicating that he had entered France illegally.

Pospishil/Nowak was induced to start talking. He confessed that he had been condemned to death in absentia by a Yugoslav court. He also had gone to Munich, and from that city to Zurich where he met Keleman, otherwise known as Vlada the Chauffeur. Pospishil was forced to admit that he had been ordered to murder the King if the first attempt failed.

Mio Kral, youngest of the defendants, told the court that he had returned to Yugoslavia after a few years' stay in Brazil. An Ustacha agent had recruited him and he had enthusiastically joined the organization. He had been picked up by the police in Klagenfurt, Austria, and charged with vagrancy. Kral admitted that he had gone to Aix-en-Provence with Keleman/Vlada and there waited for further orders from his leader. He said that a man named Petar, who was really Pavelich, had given him a Mauser revolver and bombs and told him and Vlada that they had been chosen to make the first attempt on the King's life. So far, so good: Kral was corroborating the facts uncovered by the investigators. Kral told the court that he had returned to Aix after Vlada had assassinated the King.

Then he suddenly tried to sound like a humanitarian: When the motorcade had approached, he said, Vlada had shouted, "The King is coming. One of us will have to kill him."

"I didn't want to shoot because of so many women and children. If the King had been alone I would have thrown a bomb at him. I went back to Aix. It was exactly 4:45 P.M. when I arrived there."

The police later claimed that no one had seen Kral in Aix until 6:30 P.M.

All defendants admitted that the purpose of the Ustacha was to establish an independent Croatia. They said Pavelich had told them that it was his intention to create a state of fear and anxiety throughout Europe, and the more murders the Ustacha committed the more likely the statesmen would, through fear, agree to grant freedom to Croatia.

Saint-Auban now began to deliver a very long discourse about self-sacrificing patriots ready to give up their lives for freedom. Croats were being exploited and victimized by the primitive Serbs, and Pavelich, an innocent man, had been condemned to death in absentia because he had made a speech advocating a separate Croat state. The lawyer declared that the assassins were patriots like the French during their great revolution, fighting for liberty, equality, and fraternity. When the spectators in the courtroom roared their disapproval of his remarks, the presiding judge murmured, "Heroes! I know only that they committed a crime of common law."

Saint-Auban was not fazed one bit by the reaction of the spectators. He still insisted that the Ustacha were "freedom fighters and passionate patriots. The accused," he said, were "Croatian migrants who had come to Hungary to find gainful employment and some badly needed rest." Their pursuits were "innocent agricultural work."

Which made the defendant Pospishil snarl: "If one considers shovels and hoses as rifles, I'm sure it is due to the fact that fear has caused his mind to go overboard."

In summing up, the procurator-general mentioned that a large amount of cash had been handed over to Pavelich, and one could only guess at its origin. He would not have had to guess too hard. He knew that the funds for the Ustacha had been provided by Mussolini. But the heavy hand of Laval had effectively closed the mouths of the procurator-general, the president of the court, and everyone else in authority.

"The terrorist of yesterday," Saint-Auban fatuously ranted, "is often the government of tomorrow." Which didn't speak much for any government. He reminded the court that the men in the Kremlin had been terrorists in their day.

Loison instructed the jury that the accused were not dedicated men ready to lay down their lives for a just cause. They had no country; it did not exist. The men were common mercenaries who had been presented with expensive suits, good food, luxurious accommodations, and a large amount of pocket money. They had also been promised a very large reward upon completion of their assignment. Loison could have revealed who was paying for the job, but that was dangerous; it would open too many doors. Laval had ordered the court to keep the facts well hidden, and since the Foreign Minister was not the kind of man with whom one could trifle, Loison decided that discretion was the better part of valor.

The president of the court let the veil slip a bit when he said, "From the beginning of 1934 certain Croatian publications in Berlin uttered threats against King Alexander and Barthou. These threats have now been realized." The article to which Loison referred appeared in an Ustacha paper published on August 16, 1934. He pointed out that the article had accused the King, Barthou, and Titulescu of pursuing a policy of putting people under the yoke and that the day would come when, upon orders of the leader, "the Croatian people would awaken and take up weapons to wash off the shame in blood." Shades of Mussolini!

The defendant Pospishil suddenly cried out, "I haven't read this article, but it is truly and wholly in the spirit of the Ustacha."

The president of the court could have pulled the entire curtain aside and announced to the press of the world that Italy had been the supporter of assassins. He could have said that Hitler had conferred with Ivan Mikhailov, the leader of the I.M.R.O., and Ustacha bigwigs at the Adlon Hotel in Berlin as far back as 1929. And he could have revealed that the meeting had been presided over by the notorious Manfred Killenger, one of the men responsible for the murder of Walter Rathenau. There was an obvious connection between the Ustacha, the Nazis, and the Fascists, but Loison wasn't going to go into that story.

While Loison was silent, Saint-Auban had a good deal to say. He denounced the court for permitting "abnormal" pro-

ceedings. This was true as far as it went. But the "abnormal"
procedures were not due to the way Loison conducted the
legal aspects of the trial. He was being pressured by higher
authorities to keep certain information out of the courtroom.
Saint-Auban was well aware of all that, but he was not going
to help the prosecution. He was there to save his clients from
a death sentence. He quoted out of context from a number of
Hungarian documents, and gave a garbled version of a League
of Nations paper on the assassination. Italy, he said, was justified in refusing to have Pavelich extradited to France. The
Croat, according to him, was only trying to free his country.

"When," he asked, "in the history of mankind, was it possible to win freedom without resorting to violence?"

He said that Stephen Radich, the leader of the Croat Peasant
Party, had been most foully murdered in the Skupshtina by a
fanatic Serb. He did not tell the court that Radich had loathed
the Ustacha and all it stood for, and that he was against any
separatist movement. The lawyer insisted that the Ustacha was
justified in seeking to avenge the murder of Radich by killing
the King.

Saint-Auban was delivering a lecture on Yugoslav and European history—as told by the defense. He spoke about the
assassination of Archduke Ferdinand and his morganatic
spouse at Sarajevo, and he wanted to know why Princip who
had committed *that* murder was called a patriot while his
three clients were stigmatized as vicious killers.

Saint-Auban's oratory did not make any impression on
Loison. After the defense attorney had finished his closing
speech, Loison asked the three defendants if they had anything to say on their own behalf. They remained silent. Loison
presented the jury with thirty-two written questions. He asked
them to give a simple yes-or-no answer on all of them.

Had there been a voluntary homicide? If the response was
affirmative, had it been premeditated? Did the Ustacha terrorists attempt to murder General Georges? Were the defendants

accessories to the crime? Did the defendant Kral assist Vlada the Chauffeur when he murdered the King and Barthou? Were Raich and Pospishil involved in the attempt?

The jury found the men guilty of most of the charges. Pospishil and Raich were held to have actively assisted Vlada and Kral in the murder of the gendarme, Galy, which they found to be unpremeditated. The three men were considered accessories to the crime.

The jury also discovered some extenuating circumstances that appeared to favor the accused. Despite this implied recommendation for mercy, Pospishil, Kral, and Raich were found guilty and sentenced to life imprisonment. When the Vichy Regime became the Government of unoccupied France, the three were set free.

Pavelich, Kvaternik, and Perchevich were tried in absentia and condemned to death by a court in Aix.

Both London and Paris were relieved when the trial ended, and well pleased with its results. The London *Times* said that Franco-Italian rapprochement had "not only stood the strain of this sorry affair, but had been reinforced" because of it.

The paper arrived at that conclusion after Laval and Baron Aloisi had had a long discussion about the future of relations between their two countries. Since the *Times* generally reflected the opinions of Whitehall, it was assumed that Stanley Baldwin and his colleagues were satisfied by the trial and the conference.

The only ones who were disgruntled were Benes, Titulescu, and Yevtich and the leaders of Greece and Turkey, who felt that the big powers had betrayed them. But Laval paid no attention to their criticisms. He could now plunge ahead on his program of appeasing Berlin and Rome.

❊   ❊   ❊   ❊

A few years after the trial, *Khrvatski Glas,* a newspaper published in Winnipeg, Canada, printed a confession by one Ante Bilankov, a Dalmatian, who said he had been recruited by Pavelich's agents and trained in northern Italy. From there he had been sent to Yanka Pusta, and eventually back to Italy.

"After six months at Yanka Pusta," his statement said, "I was sent with six others to Italy and we were detailed to the camp of Olivieto in the province of Toscana. There I met some acquaintances to whom I recounted all that had happened to me in Hungary and they said that their position in Italy was as desperate as mine. We put our heads together how to put an end to the conditions of life which had become intolerable. We were all in danger that night would devour us as the phrase went. That was no exaggeration. One of us, a student named Vlado Kunich, wrote a letter to Mussolini airing our grievances and begging his intervention on our behalf. But when Mussolini received that letter he sent it at once to Pavelich. Kunich was arrested and subjected to the most frightful tortures and then made to dig his own grave before he was killed.

"Pavelich often came to the camp and he gave orders that we rebels be transferred from the camp of Olivieto to San Demetrio in the province of Abruzzi. There we were divided into two groups and some of us were sent to Fonteccio and others to San Lorenzo. Our opinions were denounced by spies set to watch us. Pavelich gathered us together and threatened us with these words:

"'Serb blood is to me as water, but if any of you shows the slightest insubordination in camp or against officers his blood will be to me as the most stinking in the canals.'

"As a result our indignation increased and Dr. Budak (one of Pavelich's henchmen) reported a number of us as anti-Fascists and enemies of Italy. We were arrested and subjected to dreadful torture. The torture went on for seventy-two days and I am incapable of describing our sufferings. . . . Every night we were visited by inhuman tormentors and put to the question. Some of us remained for days unconscious after these visits. Some had blood poisoning and died.

"Eleven of us were condemned to death and the rest were

sent to Stromboli. There we heard that Perchets had been condemned to death for betrayal."

This article was published on April 5, 1938. All these facts about the Ustacha and Mussolini's sponsorship of it were known to both the French and the British authorities, but the men leading the two democracies decided to sweep the story under the carpet.

François Poncet, French Ambassador to Berlin, in his book *The Fatal Years*, stated that Mussolini was the man behind the killings. The Mauser used by Vlada was purchased in a Trieste shop. Weapons could not be purchased in Italy without the permission of the authorities.

Joseph Paul Boncour, Queen Marie's legal counselor, had access to the records of the judicial investigation conducted in France months after the murders had been committed. These revealed that the "real criminals, the instigators and organizers of the assassination, were in Italy."

In 1944, Baron Pompeo Aloisi was tried for his complicity in crimes that had been perpetrated by the Duce. He admitted that while he was Under-Secretary for Foreign Affairs, and was trying to effect a rapprochement with Yugoslavia, Mussolini had given secret orders to have the King murdered. "It often happened," he said, "that the Ministry of Foreign Affairs and the embassies followed a line of policy that was the opposite of the dictator's real plans. In this way he sought to deceive others and prepare alibis for himself. Shady enterprises were put into execution through cabinets and secret agencies in Italy and his ambassadors abroad obeyed his will alone. . . . (They) depended directly on the head of the Government and his Cabinet."

Alessandro Borgomanero, Commissioner of Public Security of the Ministry of the Interior, testified that the Ustacha was paid with secret funds from the Ministry of Foreign Affairs. Crospino Agostenicci, a general in the carabinieri, said that the Ustacha had a special group of his men at its disposal.

The British knew all that and more; so did the French.

Whitehall had been informed by Sir Neville Henderson, serving as Ambassador in Belgrade, that Mussolini had planned to have his ships transport hundreds of Ustacha terrorists to Yugoslavia after Alexander was killed. H. D. Harrison, covering the Balkans for British newspapers, wrote, "The assassination fleets of small ships laden with Ustacha terrorists sailed from the North Italian ports in the Adriatic to land in Dalmatia. But Henderson, personally, on his own, got in touch with the British fleet which had been on a visit to Dalmatia and was just leaving the Adriatic, and got them to sail back to Trieste. This prevented what might otherwise have been an invasion of Yugoslavia which might have made it what Spain became later on—the field for trial of weapons and strength between the dictatorships and the West."

21 The Aftermath

The world knows too well the traitorous activities of Pierre Laval during the time when Germany occupied most of France. He was arrested and jailed by the DeGaulle Government when the country was liberated. While in prison awaiting his fate, he wrote a long memorandum (dated October 2, 1945) in which he tried to convince his countrymen that he had been a patriot.

In explaining his sabotage of the Barthou policy he said, "I wanted our country to live on terms of good neighborhood with Germany. I publicly advocated a rapprochement and an entente in 1931, and relations of good neighborhood in 1935. But at the same time because I was aware of Hitler's boundless ambition and the ever growing power of his armies, because he wanted to build a great Reich and insure Germany's hegemony over Europe, I carried out a virtual encirclement of Germany. It was to that end that I signed the Rome agreements with Mussolini. It was for that reason that I facilitated the reconciliation of Italy with Yugoslavia and Roumania for her defense. It was to that end that I negotiated the Franco-Soviet Pact."

Laval was still a liar, trying to rewrite history in order to convince the world that he was only following the policy that had been laid down by Barthou. But he had put the Franco-Russian Pact on ice as soon as he took over the Foreign Ministry, trying his best to delay its ratification, and he even told some of his newspaper admirers that he hoped to kill it forever.

Laval made no bones about using the pact as a bargaining point to squeeze some minor concessions out of Hitler. Once he had arrived at an understanding with the Führer, he intended to dump Russia. The real objective was to allow Hitler a free hand in Eastern Europe. Laval later admitted to a close associate that he had "signed the Franco-Soviet Pact but it will not be ratified quickly. By then I shall have reached an understanding with the Reich."

Pertinax, highly regarded as a political writer, said in *The Gravediggers of France*, "It looked as if he had come to terms with Russia only to be able to make a better bargain with Germany."

The slippery Laval even had an explanation for his strange behavior at the Stresa Conference: "I was asked by Mr. (Ramsay) MacDonald in the face of the German danger which was growing clearer, to form a chain from London to Moscow. I had signed the Rome agreements and the Franco-Soviet Pact. They had swept away difficulties which had been deemed insurmountable. But England was not yet ready to consider that policy of encirclement of Germany which alone might have made it impossible for Hitler to become noxious and this would have prevented war."

The appeasement virus was, of course, malignant in England at the time. When Hitler was engaged in rearming the

Reich, Labourite George Landsbury wanted to "close every recruiting station, disband the army, dismantle the navy and dismiss the air force."

Prime Minister Stanley Baldwin was certain that the German Air Force did not represent a "menace" to the British. He told his countrymen that Germany's air arm was "not fifty per cent of our strength today."

In Geneva, the Frenchman who served as the League's Secretary General was completely under the thumb of Laval. It was Avenol who delayed calling a meeting of the Council when Mussolini was threatening to have his army invade Ethiopia. When a number of French officials in Geneva criticized Laval's attitude, the head of their Government told Aveneol: "It is intolerable and I shall not allow French officials at the League to raise their voices against my policies. Do you know where that will lead to, M. Avenol? We will refuse to pay our dues to the League. That is what will happen if a French Minister continues to be attacked by his own people."

Avenol took the hint and saw to it that the Council cooperated with Laval.

The logical consequences of Laval's policy led to the sellout of Ethiopia. When Haile Selassie was trying to bring the problem to the attention of the League of Nations Council, Baron Aloisi said that it was not necessary to take up the time of that body since Article Five of the Italo-Ethiopian Treaty—signed in 1928—called for direct negotiations between the two states whenever any differences occurred between them. The Duce, the good Baron assured the Council, was most anxious to work out a settlement with Ethiopia.

"It is in conformity with the spirit of the Covenant and the traditions of the League of Nations to encourage direct negotiations concerning disputes that may arise between two member states," he reminded everyone. Discussions of the Abyssinian request "would not facilitate the continuance of direct negotiations." Italy would be forced to withdraw from the League, he promised, if the Council insisted on conducting debates on the subject.

Laval and Eden knew that Mussolini could not start his invasion of Ethiopia until the weather had cleared up. The rainy season generally ended toward the fourth week of September. The modern Roman legions would be bogged down in a sea of mud if an invasion were ordered before that time. Eden now came forward with a delaying tactic. An attempt should be made, he said, to comply with Article Five of the treaty between the two feuding powers by reaching an accord through direct negotiations. If that was not possible, the Council would examine the matter.

Frederick T. Birchall, correspondent of *The New York Times,* sent a dispatch to his newspaper explaining what was behind the maneuvers of the two major powers. Mussolini, he wrote, "cannot declare war on the country, which like Italy is a member of the League of Nations, but any punitive expedition after the fashion set by Japan in China has been shown to be possible without graver consequences than a League rebuke. Apart from action by the League there is nothing to prevent Premier Mussolini from acting as he pleases toward this distant Italian colonial neighbor. It is generally understood that when the subject of recent Abyssinian conflicts came up in his conference with Pierre Laval . . . the French Foreign Minister gave the Italian Premier a free hand to carry out any police operations he cared to undertake in that part of the world. No forceful interference from Great Britain is likely either. . . . Britain, through Sir Sidney Barton, the resident minister there, therefore has been counseling the Emperor to make his peace with Italy as quickly as possible by direct negotiations."

On January 29, two days after Laval and Eden had given him the time he needed to prepare his aggression against Ethiopia, Mussolini instructed his Ambassador in London to inform the British Government that "an agreement on Ethiopia [had been] secretly reached at the beginning of the month with France." He wanted to know what the British thought of that move.

A month after Mussolini sent the note, Sir John Simon assured the House of Commons that the Duce was still interested in direct negotiations with Haile Selassie. The British Minister in Addis Ababa had been told, he said, "to use his offices in promoting the negotiations."

Sir John knew that the invasion of Ethiopia was about to begin, while Britain and France were playing fast and loose with the peace of the world.

Arnaldo Cortesi, Rome correspondent of *The New York Times*, who was considered to be pro-Fascist, wrote: "Two divisions numbering somewhere between 25,000 and 35,000 men, complete with artillery, tanks and motorized sections, were placed on a war footing and mobilized. It is said in official quarters that large quantities of ammunition and war materials of all kinds either have been or are on the way to Eritrea and Italian Somaliland. It is believed that the knowledge of the intense military preparations being made by Italy will convince the Emperor of the uselessness of resistance and help make up his mind to accept the Italian demands. If he should prove obdurate and refuse to take the necessary measures, however, then direct Italian intervention seems to be the only alternative."

And during that same period Birchall, reporting from Geneva, observed that the Council of the League and its Secretary-General appeared to be adopting an attitude of "extreme calm" about "what seems to be a somewhat urgent business. The League," he said, "is in a state of suspended animation."

When Haile Selassie asked the League to intervene in the dispute, the British Government proposed that an Inter-Departmental Committee should be organized "to study British interest in Ethiopia." The Committee discovered that the "ultimate aims" of Mussolini were "not pure and simple economic predominance, but the virtual absorption of as much of Ethiopian territory as could be absorbed without prejudicing

Italian influence in other parts of the world."

On March 22, Laval presented an agreement to the French Chamber of Deputies which, according to him, would keep Mussolini from violating "the sovereignty or the independence of Ethiopia." The deputies did not trust the sallow little lawyer; they believed that he was betraying the Ethiopians and selling out his own country into the bargain.

Laval was still prating that Mussolini was about to align his country with France at the very time the Duce was advising Chancellor Schuschnigg of Austria to join the totalitarian side: "My dear friend, we are witnessing the final crackup of the West European democracies. Austria's place is at the side of the dynamic powers. This is how you can best ensure the safety of your country."

While Laval continued trying to get Mussolini to divorce Hitler, General Badoglio told the French General Gamelin that the Duce had definitely committed his country to an alliance with the Third Reich. The Hoare-Laval deal which gave Italy a free hand in Ethiopia convinced Mussolini that the democracies had no intention of doing anything to stop aggression. Many years later, just before the Munich sellout of Czechoslovakia, he admitted that Italy would have been defeated if the League of Nations had really enforced sanctions when he waged war on Ethiopia.

After Mussolini's army had chewed up Ethiopia, and the Nazis had taken over the Rhineland, the London *Times* published an editorial entitled "A Chance to Rebuild." "The old structure of European peace, one-sided and unbalanced, is nearly in ruins," it said. "It is the moment not to despair but to effect a friendship with Germany."

Two years after Hitler had successfully executed his Rhineland coup, he had his troops march into Austria, and six months after that he was threatening Czechoslovakia. It was then that Neville Chamberlain was brave enough to take a plane (it was the first time he had flown) and arrive in Munich just in time to hand over the Sudetenland to the Reich. When Hitler asked if he had any objections to the takeover, Chamberlain replied that he "could state personally" that he "recognized the principle of the detachment of the Sudeten areas."

That appeasement led to the total takeover of Czechoslovakia toward the end of September 1938. The betrayal of a loyal ally was given the official seal of approval by Chamberlain, Daladier, Mussolini, and Hitler on September 30, 1938. On October 5, Benes resigned as President of the country and fled to England. He had been marked for killing by Mussolini and Hitler.

All the jackals were now going to take pieces out of the living body. Poland grabbed 650 square miles of Czech territory. Hungary helped herself to 7,500 square miles, and the Germans took over the rest of the country.

In their attempt to convince the populace that Hitler had to be appeased, the democratic leaders said that they needed more time to build up their armed might. Hitler, they said, was too strong. What a rationalization for betrayal and cowardice! At the Nuremberg Trials General Keitel, who as the head of the OKW was one of Hitler's favorite commanders, was asked what his military colleagues thought about the Munich Pact. His answer:

"We were extraordinarily happy that it had not come to a military operation because we had always been of the opinion that our means of attack against the frontier fortifications of Czechoslovakia were insufficient. From a purely military point of view we lacked the means for an attack which involved the piercing of the frontier fortifications."

Clear enough! Why didn't Chamberlain realize that Germany was still too weak to stand up against the democratic powers?

Field Marshal von Manstein, another Hitler favorite, said, "If war had broken out, neither our western border nor our Polish frontier could really have been effectively defended by us, and there is no doubt whatsoever that had Czechoslovakia defended herself we would have been held up by her fortifications for we did not have the means to break through."

The first step taken to appease the Fascists and the Nazis

occurred when Laval and Eden forced the Yugoslavs to cooperate with them at Geneva. The second step was taken when
Mussolini was allowed to take over Ethiopia. The third step
came when the democracies permitted Italy and Germany to
intervene in the Spanish Civil War. The rest is history.

King Alexander and Louis Barthou had been all but forgotten by the appeasers. Betrayal became a habit with the
Daladiers and the Chamberlains; they were conditioned to
give in to the dictators' demands. The men in charge of affairs
in the democracies had managed to perform a miracle: they
moved from a position of strength into a state of profound
weakness, a possibility no sane person would ever have dared
to predict.

Alexander lies today in a crypt in a church where his
Karageorgevich ancestors have also found peace. The church
is located in Shumadia, about sixty miles from Belgrade, and
many Yugoslavs still travel long distances to the mountaintop
to pay their respects to their martyred King. Louis Barthou
rests along with other French immortals in the Père Lachaise
cemetery in Paris.

People all over the world were to pay a heavy price because
the appeasers did not have the nerve or wit to stop aggression
in time. War could have been avoided if Britain and France
had followed the policies laid down by Louis Barthou, but the
pygmies who fancied themselves brilliant statesmen were bent
on soothing the Führer and his partner the Duce. They entertained a hope that the Germans would wage a war against
Russia, but the ungrateful Hitler changed his course and
attacked the West instead. The men in London and Paris
should have remembered the saying that those who dig a
grave for others will usually fall into it themselves. They, as
well as Stalin, learned that lesson too late.

Winston Churchill, once asked what the history books would
call the Second World War, said it would be labeled "the
unnecessary war." The proprietor of Chartwell saw the scene
for what it was.

Index